Godp  3

A book for godparents, godchildren, parents and churches

by John Bradford, David Gamble and Joan King

Series editor: Joan King

Written by John Bradford, David Gamble and Joan King

Rev John Bradford was Chaplain Missioner to the Children's Society for many years.
David Gamble is Family and Human Relationships Officer of the Methodist Church,
Chair of Barnardo's and a trustee of the National Family and Parenting Institute.
Joan King is a freelance writer, trainer and educator in child development and
family life education.

Series editor: Joan King

Cover design by Phillip Vernon

Published by:
National Christian Education Council
1020 Bristol Road
Selly Oak
Birmingham
B29 6LB

British Cataloguing-in-Publication Data:
A catalogue record for this book is available from the British Library.

ISBN 0-7197-0982-2

First published 2000

© 2000 John Bradford, David Gamble and Joan King

Typeset by the National Christian Education Council
Printed by Biddles, Guildford, UK

Contents

Chapter 5: Godparent Support – *for godparents*

Chapter 6: Godparents and the Local Church – *for churches*

Chapter 7: Where did the Idea of Godparents Come From?
– *some background*

Preface

This book is one in a series called *Family Options* published by the National Christian Education Council as part of its *Faith in the Future* initiative. Each book in the series focuses on options that many parents face and the choices they might make at some point in their family lives.

Shortly after a child is born, parents and their wider circle of family and friends often want to mark the occasion. Many parents from a Christian tradition choose to have their child baptised or dedicated according to the practice of their particular church or denomination. The service will help all to welcome the child into the Christian community, to thank God for the gift of this new person and to commit the child and its upbringing to parents and others 'with God's help'. If parents choose to have their child baptised or dedicated they are faced with a further important choice. Who will they choose to be godparents or sponsors of their child? After all, their child will have these godparents for a long time. This book gives guidance to parents faced with this choice and helps them to understand the role of godparents.

For those who are chosen, the prospective godparents or sponsors, there is the option of accepting the invitation or declining. It is a serious decision. This book gives guidance about the role of godparents and sponsors both on the day and afterwards as they develop their relationship with their godchild. The book emphasises that *godchildren are for life* and *being there* for them is an important part of the role. In addition, godparents themselves describe how their godchildren have enriched their lives.

This book, then, is for parents who choose godparents, for godparents who choose how to fulfil their role and for those who join them in promising to support children and their parents, i.e. local church communities and the wider family. How might they support families whose children they baptise or dedicate?

The book is also for godchildren who want to understand the promises their godparents made at their baptism or dedication to help them to know their faith story.

In this day of small families, when many children have few or no brothers and sisters and even the extended family is smaller than it was, the potential influence and significance of godparents in children's lives is increasing. As one who is thankful for a lifetime of support and friendship provided by godparents and who is also a godparent, I recommend this book. In many ways I have had to 'feel my way' as a godparent because there were few resources available to help me. My godchildren are now young adults. Having shared their lives so far, I remain convinced of the important role that godparents have in supporting them in their growing years, in sharing life and faith issues with them and in encouraging their parents as their children grow. I was, therefore, happy to collaborate with David Gamble and John Bradford in writing this book. David is currently Family and Human Relationships Officer of the Methodist Church, Chair of Barnardo's and a trustee of the National Family and Parenting Institute. John brings to the book wisdom and information gained over many years as Chaplain Missioner to the Children's Society. Together we hope that this book will provide vital encouragement and guidance for existing godparents and those who are new to the role.

Joan King
Series Editor

Introduction

Why Have we Written this Book?

Godparents have been around for centuries. While, officially, their role relates to children baptised within the Christian tradition, many people who have neither had nor been godparents and who rarely or never go to church have some idea that godparents are 'a good thing'. Perhaps it is an idea gained from seeing the 'fairy godmother' character in a pantomime like *Cinderella*. The fairy godmother fixes things so Cinderella can go to the ball and everyone (except the ugly sisters) can live happily ever after. Of course, real-life godparents cannot fix things so easily, and bear little resemblance to the pantomime character.

This book comes from the conviction that godparents are not to be confined to past centuries or pantomime stories, but can and do play an important part in the lives of real children and young people living now, in the twenty-first century. Indeed, at a time of great family change, when many people do not experience much stability and continuity in their family life, godparents can sometimes make a big difference.

As we worked on this book, we found that little had been written about godparents. We hope that what we have produced will help other people who are asking what godparents are about.

Parents

This is a book for you, whether before or shortly after the birth of your child. If you are considering having your baby baptised in a Christian church then you may also be wondering whom to invite to be godparents. Of course, you may already have chosen them or have very good ideas about whom to ask. This book will come in useful, either as you choose your child's godparents or as you think about what you are asking them to do. Chapter 1 is particularly for you while we hope you will use Chapter 3 with your child as s/he grows.

Godparents

This book is also for you, whether you are a godparent already or a prospective god-parent. It will help you think about the joys and responsibilities of being a godparent. If you are not one already, but have been invited to be one, it may help you decide whether to say yes or no to the invitation and it will certainly give you some things to discuss with the person who has asked you. If you have already said yes, or you are already a godparent, then this book may help you think about how you are getting on in the role and may offer you some new insights. Chapters 2, 4 and 5 are written particularly with you in mind.

Godchildren

This book is also for you if you are a godchild, though if you have only just become one you may not be able to read these words yet! If you are reading this as an older godchild, then Chapter 3 may help you think about the part played in your life by the people who were chosen to be your godparents when you were smaller. It may be that you know them well and they have been very important in your life. Or it may be that you rarely see them or hear from them, or even that you have lost contact with them. This book might encourage you to get in touch with them and let them know how you are getting on.

Churches

This is also a book for churches, and especially for the people in a church who have a particular care or concern for young children and their families. You may be a minister who takes baptism services. You may be someone who has special links with parents in the church or community. You may be a 'cradle roll' or 'First Steps' secretary, or the person who runs the crèche. Perhaps you are a pastoral or baptism visitor, a children's worker, or simply a member of the church who wants to make sure children are welcomed and their families supported. Chapter 6 looks at what churches can do.

Interested persons

Finally, this is a book for anyone interested in godparents. It looks at how godparenting started and how it developed (Chapter 7) and considers what godparents are for, and how that affects who might be invited to become a godparent. We look at godparents through the eyes of parents, other godparents, godchildren and the church communities in which children are baptised. We explore just some of the ways that godparents can carry out their responsibilities and develop their relationship with their godchild(ren).

So we hope you find that this is a book for you, whether you are a parent, godparent, godchild, church member or officer, or interested reader.

The contributors

The ideas in this book are not all our own. When we were writing it, as well as trying to read what had already been written on the subject, we decided to ask some real live godparents what they had done and what helpful ideas they wanted to pass on to other godparents. So we devised and circulated a questionnaire. We are very grateful to all those who returned the questionnaires, and have used many of their ideas (and some of their words) in this book. Indeed, it might be said that this book was written by over sixty people! Some godparents had only one godchild while others had several. One had ten and a married couple had fifteen between them. Most godparents seemed to have two, three or four godchildren. Some godparents told us that completing our questionnaire had encouraged them to try to re-establish a relationship with their godchild that had faded. Others found that thinking through their answers to our questions led them to a new commitment to their role. They told us of moments of joy and pain, laughter and tears, challenges and rewards. Many said they had not done the job as well as they had hoped, and felt rather guilty about it. Others had taken the role very seriously and were able to speak of some very special moments in their relationship with their godchild. Most of them had found it a privilege and responsibility to be invited to be a 'special' person in a child's life.

To all who have shared their experiences we are immensely grateful. Quite a few of them said they had not had much support and guidance when they took on the role of a godparent and felt that a book like this would have been useful. We hope you will find that this one comes up to your expectations.

Chapter 1
Choosing a Godparent

A chapter for parents

Life is never the same once a baby has been born, especially if it is the first child. Adjustments have to be made to accommodate the new, dependent member of the family. How will the household be run? What roles will the adults in the home take? What styles of parenting will the new parent(s) adopt?

There is usually a great deal of joy mixed with an 'awe-filled' sense of responsibility and a good dollop of physical tiredness thrown in. Something wonderful has happened that affects you deeply. You want to thank God for the gift of your child. You recognise your need of support in raising him or her. A baptism, or perhaps a dedication or thanksgiving service, will provide just the right occasion to bring family and friends together to celebrate the birth and ask God's blessing on the child and you. It will help your parents to recognise that they have moved up the generation ladder to become grandparents and everyone will see and know that you are now in the parent generation. Or maybe it is just the tradition in your family to have an infant baptism or dedication and it is expected of you.

Whatever your reason, when you contact the church where you hope to have your child baptised or dedicated, you will be given some guidance. Most will ask you to supply godparents or sponsors for your baby and will suggest how many. In the Anglican tradition, it is usually two godfathers and one godmother for a boy, and two godmothers and one godfather for a girl. But how will you choose the godparents for your child?

Why Casual Reasons may not be Enough

In the busyness of looking after a baby, it may even happen that the date and place of the baptism are arranged before the godparents are chosen and invited. But it is wise not to rush into making choices. Sometimes the most obvious choices are not the best. Certainly most 'off the top of the head' reasons usually prove insufficient, however reasonable they may seem at the time. Here are some:

- ○ It will keep that side of the family happy.
- ○ Can't think of anyone else.
- ○ That's someone we wouldn't squabble over.

○ Might be good if disaster struck.

○ They've done quite a bit for us – it's a way of saying, 'Thank you'.

○ Rather nice people to be associated with.

○ Won't cause us any trouble.

○ Could afford the presents.

○ Would keep the church quiet.

○ Good for a party!

Of course there may be a seed of appropriateness in any of these first thoughts. But it would be wiser to give some days to thinking things over. Start by reflecting on what qualities you might be looking for and be assured that the more carefully godparents are chosen, the greater the likelihood is of their giving good support to your child.

Here are some selection guidelines:

○ Choose after considering all close and extended **family** members as well as your wide range of *friends*.

○ Choose for the *welfare of the child* and not for the satisfaction of others.

○ Choose people who could *support* your child, their godchild, in different ways.

○ Choose those you would really want your child to *keep contact with* for life.

○ Choose *together:* father and mother need to be mutually content.

In some families the choice of godparents can become a contentious issue, a political battle. This may give you reason to look outside the family for godparents. Whoever you choose, however, it is important to remember that the invitation to become a godparent is a gift to extend to others with freedom and with pleasure, not out of a sense of duty or with serious reservations.

Some churches will provide you with a baptismal visitor who will help you talk or think through your options.

Making a Shortlist

Choosing godparents, then, is not simply a matter of 'one from your side and one from mine', or 'someone we can both get on with'. Choosing godparents takes careful consideration and time that must not be squeezed out to plan the guest list or party.

The selection guidelines given above may be applied as you, the parent(s), consider the following questions, perhaps with the helpful support of a church baptismal visitor.

11

Range

How long have you been friends? Remember, proven friends may have added value. How dependable are they? Would they be likely to carry out their role conscientiously or simply forget it once the service was over?

Welfare of the child

How do they or would they relate to and understand children? Remember, children like adults who smile and laugh, and who are fair and firm. (Obviously someone with whom the child might be in any way at risk should never be considered.)

How would they understand and relate to your child in particular? This question is particularly relevant if your child has any special needs, if there are twins, if the child is a stepchild, or if you are a 'lone' parent.

Variety

The godparents you choose, usually three, might bring different strengths, interests, insights into your child's life. Choose an interesting blend of people. Ask yourself: will one bring the strengths of being supportive to the family, will another encourage church membership and pray, will another have regular contact? You may have different criteria to apply. Decide what they are and ensure that among them the godparents can meet your criteria. You might like to consider the note below about those of other main world faiths.

An important question to consider is: will they give your child encouragement in his/her Christian journey? Are they managing their own or at least doing their best?

Contact

In choosing these people to be godparents, are you balancing godparent gender suitably? Do they understand families and have time for others?

Collaboration

Are you, the parents, listening to each other in assessing the suitability of a group of individuals to be the godparents of your child? Is this process bringing you closer together in your aims for the spiritual care of your child?

Friends and relatives from other main world faiths

Living as we do in a multi-faith society, it is increasingly the case that some parents wish to choose a godparent for their child from another world faith. Perhaps the person is a long-standing family friend or neighbour. Although such a person cannot technically take the promises of the godparent included in the baptism service for him/herself, or for the child, it may be possible for her/him to be an associate sponsor. More about associate sponsors in a moment. First let us remember that many people from other world faiths have been educated in Church Schools and have become comfortable with the Christian faith and outlook alongside their own faith and cultural tradition. They would recognise the importance of the sacrament of baptism and be diligent in supporting a growing child. We therefore suggest that, at the discretion of the priest or minister, a person from another main world faith might be invited to be a 'fourth' godparent, in other words as a named and recorded 'associate godparent' or 'associate sponsor', at their discretion. Hopefully the priest will show appropriately generous understanding and inter-faith hospitality.

Such a provision would be fitting especially where inter-faith family friendships have involved members of a Christian family attending religious ceremonies of friends from other main world faiths. However, such a step should not be taken for reasons of inter-faith courtesy alone, but for the spiritual welfare of the child. The likelihood is that an invitation to be an associate godparent would be treated very seriously indeed.

At this point it is worth noting that the proposal to have associate sponsors or god-parents fits well with the *UN Convention of the Rights of the Child, 1989* (article 29, section 29d). It describes the aims of education as, 'The preparation of a child for a responsible life in a free society, in the spirit of understanding, peace, tolerance, equality of sexes, and friendship among all peoples, ethnic, national and religious groups and persons of indigenous origins.'

On Ways of 'Asking'

Obviously it is important to think about *whom* you will choose to be the godparents of your child. Perhaps it is less obvious that thought needs to be given to *how* you will invite them. Once they have accepted the invitation and you have your group of godparents, you will also need to consider how to communicate your choice to the rest of the family.

The manner chosen to invite a friend or family member to be a godparent should be appropriate to your relationship or friendship. While it is important not to be arti-ficial, it is equally important to make the invitation special and to communicate the importance of it. 'Oh, by the way…' or some other throw-away line called across the pub floor is inappropriate. If you wish your child's godparents to take their role seri-ously then it is important to ask them in a manner that conveys the degree of importance that you place on the role. So write that special letter signed by both parents if there are two of you, or make that special telephone call, or arrange that special meal where the two of you can be present to issue the invitation.

With families becoming smaller and children having fewer aunts and uncles to sup-port them, it is becoming increasingly important to enhance the role of godparents.

So issue invitations that will affirm the godparents you have chosen to support you and your child as s/he grows in body, mind and spirit.

Looking After the Godparent

Before the baptism

Make sure that each godparent has an opportunity to meet the child with you and knows in good time about the date, time and venue. If your church offers a Baptism Preparation Group it may be possible for the godparents to join it or at least know about it. There may also be opportunities for them to meet a baptismal visitor with you when the service is explained. The role of the godparent might then be clarified.

For godparents who live at a distance you may need to supply travel and parking directions and a brief description of the church from the outside. (In a strange town it is possible to end up in the wrong building!) Encourage godparents to arrive early, possibly by arranging accommodation with family or friends nearby, and ask them to be at the church 10–15 minutes before the service begins.

At the baptism service

Try to arrange for yourself or your partner to greet the godparents and for them to sit near you. Think beforehand and brief them about any special part that they can play, such as holding the child at a certain point or receiving a candle on the child's behalf. In some churches the godparents might receive a Certificate of Baptism.

After the baptism service

Usually a lunch, tea or party is arranged. It can be a good idea to involve others in the preparation and serving of food so that you can be free to care for the baby and your guests. Sometimes it is helpful to put a beginning and ending time on the invitation so that family and friends know what is expected and the party ends before everyone is overtired and the baptism service fades into a memory. Godparents and others will appreciate thank you notes, especially if a gift has been given, and a photograph of their godchild, taken on the day, will be appreciated.

Developing the Relationship

Often godparents take their cues from the parents. How much access they are able to have to their godchild largely depends on you. They will need to know that you feel relaxed about them taking your child out for a day, or baby-sitting or accompanying him/her to church. So involve the godparents in the life of your child whenever it seems appropriate. Here are some ideas.

Birthdays

Invite godparents to their godchild's birthday parties, even if they are at a time when the godparent is unlikely to be able to attend. Feeling included is very important.

Baptismal anniversary

Invite the godparents to join you and their godchild in attending a church service on the anniversary of the baptism. It will be especially helpful if the service is at the church where your child was baptised. This annual reunion will help your child to understand what godparents are.

Christmas

Help/encourage your child to make and send cards to the godparents. When the child is very young you can send the cards, perhaps including your child's foot- or handprint or piece of scribble.

Special events

Where appropriate, invite godparents to special family events such as school sports, plays, concerts or bonfire nights, and to church events in which their godchild is taking part.

General

Do all you can to keep godparents up to date with your child's development, interests and progress. Information technology can be of assistance here and is especially useful if godparents are living some way away or if you or they move to live overseas. It is already possible for godparents to be kept up with news from their own godchildren 'on the web'.

The future

Throughout their lives, godchildren can experience their godparents as significant people who will be there for them no matter what happens. According to those who responded to the questionnaire, some of the most important moments in the relationship come when the godchildren are in their teenage years – the time when they are emotionally leaving home and the parents are letting them go. Then the godparent can be like an anchor, there as the godchild faces the challenges of Higher Education, or develops a career or commits to a long-term relationship. In short, with the encouragement of parents in the early years, a close relationship can develop between godparent and godchild that will enhance both their lives and yours.

Chapter 2
Being a Godparent
A chapter for godparents

On Ways of 'Accepting'

To be asked to be a godparent is an honour. It is a sign of friendship and trust. It suggests that you are seen as someone a bit 'special'. When you are asked to be one, a natural response is immediately to say, 'Yes, I'd be delighted.' Any sign of hesitation on your part could be disappointing for the person who has asked you. But, before taking what is quite an important step and accepting the invitation, it is worth asking yourself why you have been chosen. Why me?

Most of the godparents who answered our questionnaire said they had been chosen because they were close friends, perhaps from college or work, or relatives of one or both of the child's parents. Several suggested that an added qualification was that they were known to be active Christians and to have some understanding of faith. One said the parents saw her as *'a suitable person to act* in loco parentis *if ever that was required'*. Others were known to be good with children, or were seen to offer a good *'role model'*. Some had no children of their own but were seen as having a lot to offer as an honorary family member. One godparent had shared part of a young person's faith journey so that when that young person went for adult baptism they invited her to be a godparent. Being invited by the child rather than the parents is unusual!

Godparents are normally chosen from people of the parents' generation, but occasionally we were told of people being invited to be godparents at quite a young age (15, for example) so that the 'honorary family' role was to be more like older brother or sister than aunt or uncle.

When parents had given a lot of thought to choosing godparents, the main qualifications seemed to be someone known and liked by the parents, likely to maintain contact and interest over a number of years, often with a known but not fanatical Christian faith and commitment.

'I asked my sixteen-year-old daughter why she thought I'd been chosen – she said, "Because you are basically a happy and stable person, have strong Christian beliefs and are a good listener but are fun to be with."'

Of course, the best people to tell you why you have been chosen are the people who have asked you, most likely a parent of the child. It is not false modesty to ask them why they have chosen you, as long as you make it obvious you are not just fishing for compliments! The reason you need to know why they have asked you is so that you can take the role seriously. And that means it is important that you understand what the parents' expectations are. What kind of a godparent do they want you to be? What do they, or don't they, want you to do as a godparent? Have they thought of the implications of involving you in this way? Being a godparent is not just about having a line to say at the baptism service; it is a long-term commitment.

To Talk About

There are a number of things that you might discuss with the parent(s), such as:

○ How will you keep in touch with your godchild and get to know him/her, especially if you live some distance away?

○ How will you carry out your responsibility to provide support in the Christian upbringing of the child? For instance, it may be that you have a strong faith or a reputation for church involvement whereas the parents have not. There could be difficulties if you take your godparent role more seriously than the parents expect.

○ If you have been invited to be a godparent because you are an old friend of one of the child's parents, how does the other parent feel about the choice?

○ If you have a partner, how will they be involved on the day and into the future?

○ How will you relate to other children in the family who are not your godchildren?

Such a conversation about what you are actually being asked to do as a godparent and about how you see the role is really important, so that you can make sure your hopes and expectations and those of the parents match reasonably well. Then your godparenting can be supportive of both your godchild and the parents.

What Kind of Godparent will you be?

When you have accepted the invitation to become a godparent, spend some further time thinking about what kind of a godparent you want to be. Read the rest of this book, especially this chapter, and consider its implications. You may find it helpful to talk to other people who are godparents already.

If you have godparents yourself, think about how they have undertaken the role. Consider ways in which they made you feel special, ideas that you would like to copy, and things you would do differently.

One final thing, for the moment at least! It may seem too obvious even to mention it, but now is a good time to make sure to note in your diary both your godchild's birthday and the date, time and place of the baptism. You need to be there and you do not want to miss it!

Fulfilling the Expectations of the Faith Community

As a godparent, you have a role to play on the day of your godchild's baptism. This means being at the church in good time, sitting with the family of your godchild, and standing with the parents at certain moments in the service. Most likely, you will also have some words to say, normally in response to a question from the person taking the service. It is worth checking out at a preparatory meeting, at a rehearsal, or before the service begins, precisely what you are expected to do and where you are expected to sit, stand, move and so on. At some point in the proceedings, you may be invited to hold a candle or even hold the baby. The more prepared you are, the better. And if you have words to say, practise them so they come easily.

Of course, your commitment does not end at the close of the baptism service. Whatever else a godparent is for, a major part of the role has to do with encouraging the godchild to grow and develop in the Christian faith. The 1662 *Book of Common Prayer* gave detailed instructions on how this was to be done. Godparents were to make sure that the child heard sermons and learned the Creed, the Lord's Prayer and the Ten Commandments 'and all other things which a Christian ought to know and believe to his soul's health; and that this child may be virtuously brought up to lead a godly and a Christian life,' and then be brought to the Bishop to be confirmed. Then the major responsibility had been achieved.

More recent services are less detailed about what godparents are supposed to do, but it is still clear that helping the child grow in the Christian faith is central to their role. In the *Alternative Service Book*, the priest outlines the duties of parents and godparents as follows:

'Children who are too young to profess the Christian faith are baptised on the understanding that they are brought up as Christians within the family of the Church. As they grow up, they need the help and encouragement of that family, so that they learn to be faithful in public worship and private prayer, to live by trust in God and come to confirmation. Parents and godparents, the children whom you have brought for baptism depend chiefly on you for the help and encouragement they need. Are you willing to give it to them by your prayers, by your example, and by your teaching?' The godparents reply, 'I am willing'.

So, encouraging godchildren by prayers, example and teaching seems a simple description of what is involved in being a godparent and it is reflected in what godparents told us in their answers to our questionnaire.

Prayers

One godparent suggested the main task was *'to pray for the child daily'*; another saw it as *'to pray for children and parents'*. Yet another spoke of sometimes saying prayers with godchildren *'alongside my own children'*. There may be opportunities for the godparent to say bedtime prayers with the godchild, particularly if asked to baby- or child-sit, or if the godchild comes to visit for a weekend or holiday. Being a godparent then involves *'supporting the children with prayer and encouraging them to grow and to become confirmed.'*

Example

In one sense, being an example to a godchild is a tall order and very demanding – showing *'an example of Christianity lived out in an ordinary life'*. It raises questions about the godparent's own faith, practice of prayer, sharing in the church's worship, and lifestyle. It is not that you have to be perfect or a 'plaster saint', but your new responsibilities suggest you will be a person who takes faith seriously. Yet there must be a lot of truth in what another godparent said: *'Children develop their awareness of love and of God by being loved, accepted, supported, encouraged and by having role models of those around them.'*

Teaching

In some ways it is even harder to *'try to educate the child in the Christian faith'*; *'to do my part in helping to nurture the child, especially in faith so that the child might come for confirmation at a time chosen by him or her.'*

How do we 'teach' somebody else the Christian faith, especially if we are not very confident about it ourselves? There may be some very specific ways a godparent can help a godchild learn about the Christian faith and its story. Godparents often give presents like Bibles, books of Bible stories, Christian videos and so on. Some godparents send presents or try to visit their godchild at important times in the church year – because they are reminders of the great moments of the Christian story. Advent cards, candles or calendars; Christmas cribs; pancakes on Shrove Tuesday; palm crosses; hot cross buns on Good Friday; eggs at Easter – all these provide opportunities to remind your godchildren about you and about the Christian story. Another good idea is to send a card on the anniversary of the child's baptism. Godchildren are likely to receive lots of cards on a birthday, but far fewer on this important anniversary.

Church involvement

As godchildren grow older, they may attend worship at church or become part of a Junior Church or Sunday School. If they do not do this as part of their family, it is an area for sensitive discussion with parents. This is, after all, something in which you, the godparent, have promised to offer them support. As well as knowing a certain amount about the Christian faith, it would help to have some idea of how faith develops. (See *How Faith Grows*, which gives a reasonably simple outline of this.) At the same time it is important to remember that faith is not some separate part of life. The basic nurture that a child receives provides the building blocks for faith – things like experiencing the world as a good place, being 'special', accepted, loved, trusted, and forgiven...

Good relationships

Children (and adults) learn a lot by asking questions. If a godparent creates a good relationship with a child, then the godparent may become an adult with whom that child will discuss important questions. One godparent described this as *'to try to build a relationship with the godchild (as well as the rest of the family) that would encourage and enable taking faith questions seriously.'*

Christian nurture

The question asked of godparents in a Methodist baptism service is, 'Will you help these parents to nurture their children in the Christian faith?' The godparents reply, 'With God's help we will.' Perhaps this comes close to what the whole thing is about – praying for the child and the family, trying to set an example, helping the child to think about God and what faith means. One godparent said: *'I felt at first that I "ought" perhaps to offer instruction in the Christian faith, but over time I have come to see it as rather being in setting an example and in showing a supportive interest in the child's growth and development.'*

Nurturing the child in the Christian faith is at the heart of godparenting. It certainly is not always easy. It has to be done with sensitivity, especially if the godparent is much more actively involved in the life of the Christian community than the child's parents.

If you find this aspect rather daunting, especially if you have little or no understanding of or commitment to the Christian faith yourself, it is important to think about how you can take your promises seriously. This is one of the reasons why the Roman Catholic and Anglican Churches prefer godparents to be baptised and confirmed church members. But no one knows it all already. Being asked to be a godparent is a good moment to 'take stock' of your own development in faith. Are there books you could read, or people you might talk to? Why not go along to the church where the baptism will be held and try to get some insight into what makes the Christian community there tick?

Some Ideas from Godparents

Godparents responding to the questionnaire have suggested the following as proven helpful ways of supporting and nurturing godchildren:

○ Send baptismal anniversary cards.

○ Send each year a birthday card saying, 'Remember that you are baptised'.

○ If the child shares the name of a saint, send a card on that saint's day.

○ Display a card from the baptismal church plus the latest photo of your godchild as an aide-mémoire for prayer.

○ Encourage the family to light a baptism candle on the anniversary of the baptism.

○ Give presents, some of a Christian nature but not all – it can get boring!

○ Give Christian books, such as the Narnia series, occasionally and read stories to godchildren.

○ Provide an Advent candle, or an Advent calendar with Christian pictures or symbols rather than chocolate.

○ Give books, symbols, music, Bible reading aids appropriate to their age.

○ Give a Bible or a prayer book – *'My godson has taken his Bible everywhere when in the forces.'*

○ Subscribe to a Christian comic for a teenage godchild.

○ Be around at Christmas to help them to prepare.

○ Make an Easter garden.

Affirming your Godchild

Most of the godparents who answered our questionnaire wrote about the importance of building a relationship with their godchildren, offering general support and being interested in them. They tried *'to take an ongoing interest in the life of the child'*, *'to be a friend – a "special" someone who'd always be there.'* To them it was about being *'a "special" person – not just a relative or a friend of their parents. Someone who can develop a different relationship with the child.'* It was *'being another stable and friendly adult who can be approached and confided in if necessary.'*

But how does a godparent build this different, 'special' relationship? It can start very early – indeed, a parent may invite you to be a godparent even before the baby is born. You may be one of the first people to meet the new baby and start to get to know him or her. At the baptism you play an important role, both at the service and at any get-together after it.

If you live relatively close and are a trusted friend or relative, baby-sitting helps the relationship grow from a very early age. As the months and years pass, your relationship will depend on being interested in the child, having time for and with them, listening to them. As one godparent wrote: *'I made a point of learning as much as I can about his life, school, joys and difficulties.'* It is important to be sensitive as your godchild grows, especially if you live further away and do not see him or her very often. Do not just remember him/her as a baby. Try to keep up to date with how they are growing and developing (photographs help), their likes and dislikes, and the things they are really interested in and excited by.

When writing about the affirmation of godchildren, some wrote:

'I thought it was about making certain promises on this child's behalf, remembering birthday and Christmas presents, and trying not to embarrass the child by saying things like, "Haven't you grown?" and "When you were little you used to…"'

'Make seeing them fun, invite them to stay or have a meal with them, especially on their own. It makes them feel grown-up. Take them out to fun things. It needn't be expensive – a local street event such as carol singing at Christmas or the local church fête in summer, visits to parks and gardens and story time at libraries.'

'To take an interest in the child throughout his/her life. To be a listening ear if things get difficult with parents.'

It is not always easy to maintain and strengthen the relationship, especially if you or your godchild's family move away or if you see less of each other as your lives move in different directions. But it is important and normally possible to maintain contact, even at a distance. Some godparents keep a calendar on their wall or noticeboard, with some event or idea for every month – it is not hard to think of ways to keep in touch. Some ways were suggested earlier in the chapter. More are included in the list below alongside activities that might be undertaken if you are able to spend time with your godchildren.

Quite a lot of the godparents who answered our questionnaire said that one of the most rewarding things about being a godparent had been seeing the relationship with the godchild mature into *'long-term friendship into adulthood'*. One said some of her most precious moments were *'adult to adult with my grown-up goddaughter – seeing the sights of London and talking future career plans – hers, over a lunch. Remember holding her as a 6-week-old baby!'*

A–Z of Things to do and Places to go with a Godchild During the First 16 Years

A Art, producing it or looking at it in galleries.

B Birthday cards and presents on their birthday or yours; bookshop visits.

C Christmas cards and presents; concerts; cafés; chatting; cinema; cathedrals; computers.

D Driving lessons – giving, or paying for the first one.

E E-mail.

F Fishing; football; finance towards education or fun, e.g. *'£250 now, instead of waiting until I die!'*

G Gardens – perhaps visit one, or send seeds to grow.

H Holidays; hobbies; helping with homework.

I Ice-skating.

J Journeys.

K Knitting; kite-flying.

L Legacy; letters.

M Meals – out or in; museums.

N Nappy-changing when they are babies.

O Overnight stops.

P Phone; postcards when on holiday or travelling.

Q Quiet times together.

R Reading stories.

S Stop-overs; silly faxes; special events; steam train trips; school plays and assemblies; sledging; swimming.

T Treats; theatre; TV; tucking them up in bed; ten pin bowling.

U Umpiring tennis or cricket matches.

V Visits; videos – home-made ones are good for sending messages from a distance.

W Walks.

X Xylophone-playing or other musical activity beginning with an easier letter!

Y Youth hostelling.

Z Zoo visit.

Encouraging the Parents

Parents invite people to become godparents because they want them to be 'special' to their child. But they probably do it also because they see you as, or would like you to be, 'special' to them too. Godparents often have an existing and long-term friendship with one or both parents, so in the early days you are more likely to relate to parents than children, especially around the time of the birth of the baby. You may be invited to share the excitement and anticipation, the worry and possibly fears before the baby is born. If you are already a parent and this is their first child, you may be able to offer moral support and reassurance.

When the baby has been born, you will probably be able to visit to meet the baby and family, especially if there are arrangements to be made for the baptism day. It is certainly worth visiting if at all possible when you are invited to be a godparent – not least so that you can talk about your expectations and understandings of what you are being asked to do.

On the day

On the baptism day itself, your presence will be appreciated and there may be all kinds of ways you can help out and give support. As a godparent, you may be able to bring order out of chaos and look after young siblings or cousins, chat to aunts, uncles and grandparents and more distant friends and relatives.

You may give a present to your godchild. You could give something significant – a baptismal gown, a candle, a Bible (if so, choose carefully – one that can be used rather than one that is just for show), a prayer book, a book of stories. Or you might give something useful – something for the baby to wear, to eat from, to sleep in, or even money or a savings account to which you add a little each year until your godchild is eighteen or twenty-one. Alternatively, you might choose something precious like a silver mug, some jewellery, such as a bracelet, chain, or cross. A baptism present does not have to be expensive, but it will be especially appreciated if you have obviously thought carefully about finding something appropriate.

As well as giving presents to the baby, you may decide to bring presents for the parents. Of course, clothes or equipment for the baby are very useful. But a tired parent trying to cope with sleepless nights may also be very happy to be pampered by being given something especially for them. Or you might decide on something linked with your particular role as godparent. There are some useful books for parents to help them think about their role in developing their child's faith, such as *Praying with sticky fingers*, *Milestones*, or *It's a very special day*. For further information see the list of resources at the back of this book.

After the baptism

You will need to find your own ways of keeping in touch with the parents as their child grows. If you live nearby, you may be able to offer very practical help – coming and providing company, or being an extra person to prepare and administer bottles or change nappies, especially where there are twins! You are likely to be one of the first people entrusted with baby-sitting. This service is appreciated by parents and helps develop your relationship with your godchild. One godparent *'looked after him when his parents went to house-hunt for the weekend.'*

Many godparents identified support for parents as central to their role, both in the Christian upbringing of the child and in more general ways: *'to support and encourage parents with the parenting'*; *'to keep contact as far as practicable with parents and children'*; *'to support the parents in bringing up the child as a Christian through prayer and friendship'*.

'A godparent is someone who supports parents in their role with prayer and love. It is another adult who is valued by children and adults, who can stand outside situations, have ideas bounced about with, and love and care and pray for those concerned.'

Godchildren come from all kinds of families. They may have one parent figure or two. These may be birth parents, step-parents or adoptive parents. It may have been a difficult birth and the mother may have been ill at the time of the birth or may experience post-natal depression for several months after it. The pregnancy may have been unplanned and the family may not have the space or money easily to take on another member. Your godchild may have been born with a life-threatening illness or some kind of physical or learning disability. The child may later have an accident or may be the victim of 'cot death', in which case the parents will be devastated and you may be much needed. The different kinds of support you will be able to offer, and the question of whether you are the right person to offer it, will depend on trying to understand factors such as these.

Support through parenting groups

Being a parent is no easy job. The hours are long and the training and support, let alone pay, severely limited. Many parents have found it helpful at times to join a group with other parents and maybe follow a parenting course of a few weeks. The group helps them to think about the kind of parent they want to be and to develop appropriate skills for being such a parent. Churches often run such courses, as, sometimes, do schools and other community groups. Seeking help to become a better parent is not a sign of weakness and failure. Rather, it is a sign that a person is taking the role seriously and wants the best for the child. Some godparents may feel able to encourage their godchildren's parents to join such a group.

Over the years there may well be times when the parents very much appreciate you 'being there' for them and their child. Godparents wrote to us of offering *'support of one or both parents, especially through tough times'*. They said they had *'been a sounding-board for parents and hopefully encouraged them in their parenting'*, and described themselves as people *'with whom parents and children can let off steam about one another (but usually separately).'*

Interventions

As a godparent, you will have to think carefully about when and how to intervene if things get tough or if, for any reason, you disagree with a parent's approach. *'There have been times when I have wanted to speak, e.g. about a parenting intervention, but have felt it important to keep quiet. There have also been times when I have spoken when it would have been more helpful if I had kept quiet.'* Possible causes of conflict include the situation where a parent is much less committed to the Christian aspects of your godparenting task than you are. Another would be where a parent has high hopes that the child will 'follow in their footsteps' or achieve an ambition the parent always held but never achieved, but where the child's interests lie in a different direction altogether. Yet another would be if a parent is at his/her wits' end with a teenage child who is staying out all night, being bullied at school, becoming involved in crime or drugs, or 'living it up' and doing little or no work at school or university. Godparents might be approached by either a parent or a god-child to have a talk with the other person. Godparents: take care!

Child abuse

A word should be said here about child abuse. We know that many children experi-ence their home as a very unsafe or unsupportive place. Different people will have different views on what constitutes 'abuse'. For example, there is a whole spectrum of belief about the appropriateness of the physical punishment of children. As we write, the Government has begun a consultation process on the matter. It is a very hard thing to decide what to do if you believe your godchild is being neglected or subjected to emotional, physical or sexual abuse. Would you tackle a parent about it? If so, how? At what point would you seek outside help?

Getting this right is very difficult, especially if you are a long-term friend of a par-ent whom you now feel to be treating a child badly. But, in the end, the safety of the child is the most important thing. Parents do not always have the same interests as their children. Sometimes they can be unaware of the effects of their actions on their children, especially when they are having a hard time themselves: for exam-ple, work pressures, unemployment, health or financial worries, their own adult relationships, or domestic violence. You are committed to the well-being of your godchild. If you are concerned, then seek help!

Being an 'Anchor'

W hen it came down to it, many godparents defined their role as 'being there' for their godchild and the family. Hopefully that means 'being there' for lots of good times and special moments. It also means 'being there' over the years as the godchild grows and develops and the relationship deepens and matures. There may also be harder times. We have hinted at some of those in this chapter and we shall return to it in greater depth in Chapter 4.

It will not always be easy to keep contact with a godchild, but our godparents suggested it was worth trying, with regular gentle reminders that you are 'there' and that you see them as 'special'. Sometimes it means being very sensitive and even holding back: *'Keeping the special godparent relationship and a different but special relationship with the other children can be difficult, especially if the godparents of the other children see and fulfil their role differently from you.'*

'Godparenting can be challenging as families grow and change.'

But if you work at it, then when times are difficult for your godchild you may be for them what one godparent described as an 'anchor' and another as a 'safe haven'.

Baptism Anniversary Gifts

O ne way of working at the relationship with a godchild and of communicating the importance of the baptism to both of you is to give a small gift on the anniversary of the baptism. This is something that can be done even if it is difficult to sustain more regular contact. Remembering to do this each year, and ensuring that the gift is in some way related to your shared Christian heritage, will help your godchild to understand your role and make links with the Christian faith.

Below are some ideas of gifts that you may obtain from a shop specialising in selling religious books and artefacts – or the church bookstall may be able to help you.

Year 1:   A toy with bells

Year 2:   A 'goodnight' prayer book, such as Ladybird

Year 3:   An audio tape or CD of children's hymns and songs

Year 4:   A Bible story jigsaw puzzle

Year 5:   A small wooden cross or candlestick

Year 6:   An illustrated Bible with reasonably large print

Year 7:   A religious picture or poster

Year 8:   A recorder or simple musical instrument such as an ocarina

Year 9:   A subscription to a children's Bible reading aid/notes

Year 10: A video with a theme related to the Good News, such as *The Miracle Maker*

Year 11: An anthology of Christian prayers

Year 12: A friendship bracelet or a mug or plate relating to a Christian 'cause', such as the debt campaign, the local church, relief of poverty

Year 13: A book of questions and answers about the Christian life

Year 14: A biography or autobiography of a Christian pioneer or leader

In addition, Easter cards, and Advent calendars illustrating the Christmas story, will help to reinforce your godchild's Christian identity in a personal way. Keeping in touch in this way need not be expensive but it can have a profound effect in low-key ways.

Chapter 3
Having a Godparent
A chapter for godchildren

For Adult Godchildren

If you have godparents yourself, you may like to consider the role that they have had and continue to have. You will have known them all your life and you probably find that you related to them differently as you grew up. When you were a child they related to you as a child; when you were a teenager you may have found you could talk to a godparent in a way that you did not do with your parents. As an adult you may have found that you have special bonds with godparents who were there for you in your childhood and teenage years. It may be that you have lost contact with one or more of them as you have grown. So pause and...

Recall your godparents

Think about each in turn – their different personalities, the times you spent with them at different stages of your life, any special moments, any special gifts given to mark particular events in your life, a time when one of them listened to you or remembered you.

○ In what ways did they support you in exploring questions of faith and in getting to know the Christian story?

○ Where are they now? What part, if any, do they play in your life now?

○ How do you try to include them in your life now?

○ How has 'having godparents' made a difference to you?

○ If you were asked to be a godparent, in what ways would you want to be like them and in what ways would you want to be different from them?

Godchildren's Questions

It may be that you have children of your own and chose godparents for them. During their primary school years they are likely to have some questions, such as: Why do I have godparents? Why did you choose these particular people to be my godparents? What promises did they make? What follows has been written particularly so that children might be helped to have a better understanding of the godparent relationship.

A Special Relationship

Godparents are Very Important People. You probably have three, two men and one woman if you are a boy, and two women and one man if you are a girl. They are important and special because they have been chosen by your Mum or Dad, or both of them, to be your godparents. They did not apply for the job. They did not get it because they are your aunt or uncle or Granny or whoever. They were specially chosen because they were the people your parent(s) wanted to be your special grown-up friends now and throughout your life. They looked at them and said, 'Yes, they're the ones.'

So they asked them: 'Will you be godparents for ....?' And they said, 'Yes'. In fact they were probably pleased to be asked. They thought that you were 'cool' and maybe you could have some good times together. And they thought that you were so important, so valuable that they would go to church and promise to remember you in their prayers – because that is one of the things that godparents do.

Can you remember your baptism? Probably not. Most of us were too young when it happened to us. If so, ask someone older who was there to tell you what happened. Here are some questions to ask, if you have not done so already:

○ When was I baptised?

○ Where was I baptised?

○ What was the water used for at my baptism?

○ What was the special Christian sign that the minister made? Why did s/he make this sign?

○ What promises were made? Who made them?

○ Are there any photographs that were taken on the day? If so, can I see them?

You and any other children being baptised that day were the most important people at the party. Everyone came to the church for it because they were glad that you had arrived and they wanted to thank God for your landing or birth. Then, in front of everyone, your godparents were asked if they would support your parents in bringing you up. They were asked to do this by being there for you and helping you to know about Jesus and what it means to be one of his followers. Together they answered using words like these: 'With God's help we will.'

So with God's help your godparents try to be special to you, praying for you, remembering important days like birthdays – though you may need to forgive them if they miss the day. Usually they will make up for it at another time. They try to be there for you, even if it is by telephone or e-mail, so that you can talk to them if you want to or share a joke or get some help with homework. Godparents are supposed to have big ears so that they can listen a lot. Have you looked at your godparents' ears lately?

Something to do

Look at some photographs of your godparents. Think about each godparent. Each will be special to you in a different way. One might see you more than the others because s/he lives nearby. Another might know a lot about football or your favourite video and chat on the phone about it. Another might take you out for a treat sometimes. Think of one thing about each godparent that you want to say 'thank you' for. Then say 'thank you' to God for your godparents who were chosen especially for you and ask God to go on helping them.

Someone to Share With

Perhaps one of the most important things a godparent does is to be there for you – when times are good and when they are not. They like to hear about what you are doing, what you are interested in and if there is anything that you are troubled about. You might find one of your godparents easier to talk to than the others. That's OK. The best ones to talk to when you have a problem are those who are good at listening, the ones with the big ears, and who know when to keep their mouth shut. After all, you do not want all your secrets or troubles to be shared around.

Sometimes it is good to listen to your godparents – not just when you want a bit of advice. They are usually interesting people and they know a lot, like how to mend a puncture on your bike, or how to solve a mathematics problem or the words of the latest CD. Think about some of the special things that your godparents like to do, their interests and hobbies. It may be that they share one of them with you. Here are some interests that some godparents have shared with their godchildren:

- ○ Football or hockey
- ○ Line dancing
- ○ Going to the library and choosing books
- ○ Going to the park
- ○ Feeding ducks
- ○ Watching the latest film
- ○ Swimming

Having a Godparent

○ Going to church
○ Washing the car
○ Gardening
○ Taking photographs
○ Involvement in a campaign, such as for debt relief

Can you think of any special interests that your godparents have shared with you?

Some godchildren find that their godparents, or at least one of them, have been there for them when life has been hard:

'My godmother came to look after us when my baby sister was in hospital.'

'I talked to my godfather when I was dropped from the school team.'

'When Granny died, my godmother was there. She didn't say much – she was just there and it helped.'

Some godchildren have found that their godparents have been there when times have been good:

'We went to the seaside and both ate candy floss when we were on the beach.'

'My godmum came on holiday with us and we had loads of fun.'

Some godchildren have found that their godparents have been there when they have had a question. They do not always know the answers to your questions but they will usually let you ask them when you are ready and help you to find some answers.

So whether you are in good times or in bad times, whether you have an important question to ask or a problem to solve, or if you just want to share a joke with someone who thinks you are special, then –

Make sure you have your godparents' telephone numbers handy.

A Help in Looking Outwards

As you get to know your godparents better you will probably find that they are OK people, people you can trust who ask questions like, 'How's your team doing?' or 'What are you making?' or 'Did you see...?' or 'What do you think about...?' Sometimes they give you choices like 'Would you like to do this ... or that ... for a birthday treat?' rather than deciding for you. After all, your godparents were chosen because they would be OK, special and trustworthy.

Your godparents were chosen because they will love you and care for you no matter what happens. They recognise that you are God's gift to your parents and that God loves you very much. Sometimes they will help you to think about God and the world that God made. They will often join you in helping to make the world – which is a bit sad and rather spoiled at present – into a better place.

'My godparents gave me lots of stuff for the Blue Peter Jumble Sale.'

'We both have collecting boxes and the money from them is sent to help provide water taps in villages where the women walk miles every day to get enough water for their families to drink.'

'We did a sponsored walk for...'

Sometimes godparents will give you a book or a small gift that helps you to think about your Christian faith – perhaps a Bible story book, a jigsaw puzzle or a little wooden cross. Don't be surprised if they do. One of the promises they made at your baptism was that they would help you to know Jesus' story and what it might mean for you.

'Every Easter we make an Easter Garden and my godmother tells me the Easter story while we do it.'

People are different. You may find that some of your friends have not been baptised or that they and their families belong to a different religion. Your parents or godparents may help you to explore some of your questions about the religions that your friends belong to – they might find books at the local library or ask the parents of your friends to explain.

Your parents, supported by your godparents, have chosen to bring you up in the Christian Church. They and other church members will want you to know how special you are to God. They will help you to explore what it means to be a Christian who believes in:

○ God the **Father** who made the world

○ God the **Son** (Jesus) who died to save the world and

○ God the **Holy Spirit** who is with us to help us.

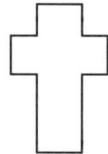

Someone to 'Include'

By now you will have got the message that your godparents are there for you. They are not your parents but 'parent' forms part of their name. They are certainly not God but 'god' forms part of their name. If you think about it, a name like 'godparent' must be special, deep and meaningful. Your godparents have been chosen by your parents and by the church to be close and special to you, to be wise, fun friends, to be there when you need them, to pray for you, and to help you know the story of the Christian faith. They may not all be able to do all of those things but they will all be able to do some of them.

But godparents are not just there for you. There is a sense in which you are there for them. It is hard for godparents to be your friends, to be available for you if you are not a friend of theirs who wants to include them in your life sometimes. So think of the ways you have shown your godparents that you are their friend and love them. There may be other things that you could do. Here is a list made by some godchildren:

○ Make a birthday card and post it.

○ Invite them to your birthday party.

○ Phone them up for a chat.

○ Send a postcard when you are on holiday or on a school trip.

○ Paint a picture for them.

○ Give them a copy of your school photograph.

○ Ask them to come to your school fête or sports day.

○ Invite them to watch a video, or read a story, or watch a match with you.

○ Remember them in your prayers.

You might be able to think of other things to add to the list.

When you include your godparents by doing things with and for them, they feel special. And you know how important it is to feel special and loved in this way.

Chapter 4
Godparenting at Special Moments

A chapter for godparents

Special Days

'I have had ongoing contacts over 35–40 years: birthdays, Christmas, new school, celebration of awards, times of change, marriage, parenthood, etc.'

An obvious opportunity for a godparent to contact a godchild by phone, letter or e-mail, or to 'be there' in person, is on a special or significant day in the godchild's life – a birthday, anniversary, or 'rite of passage'. Some godparents describe their experiences:

'When she had her 21st birthday party I was asked to say a few words.'

'I received and accepted their wives/husbands, welcomed their children.'

'When the eldest godchild, a student, was visiting student friends in Manchester she wanted to bring all her mates around to meet me!'

'When the eldest (now 12) starts clubbing I hope she will let me come along!'

In *Milestones,* Judy Jarvis, Christine Elliott Hall and Mary Jefferson show how special days, both good and bad, can start early in a child's life. It is worth considering how to mark their significance and remind a child that they are special. Early special days include when a new baby arrives in the home or is baptised (when the older child may feel left out), the first night away from parents, starting school and so on. The special days continue throughout life and can be marked sometimes quite simply with a telephone call or a card.

'I try to send "good luck" type cards if he is taking exams or tests. (He is learning to play the cello.)'

'When my first godchild got good exam results after a struggle, I was the first person he wanted to tell.'

'I was invited by my eldest godson to meet him off his ship when he came back from Kosovo – I felt touched that he wanted me there.'

Days to remember are: exam results day, whether good or bad; graduation day; starting a new job; doing well at sport, music or hobbies. Further special events to mark include: passing a cycling proficiency or driving test; finding a partner; getting married; moving into a new home; becoming a parent – even though the latter may make you feel old, as a 'god-grandparent'!

In Chapter 2 we also suggested that a godparent could make a point of marking 'special days' in the Christian year – Advent, Christmas, Shrove Tuesday, Ash Wednesday, Lent, Palm Sunday, Easter, Pentecost, saints' days, etc. The baptism anniversary is a 'churchy' event that is special for your particular godchild.

Remember, too, that sometimes it seems as if we are only concerned about 'success' in a very narrow sense, linked with high achievement. Not all godchildren will achieve in this sense, indeed most of them will not, at least most of the time. Some do not have particular abilities that obviously mark them out from other people. Others may have ability but they had a bad day or did not make an effort. They may have 'failed' deliberately, possibly to show their parents that they want to live their own lives, rather than simply follow the course charted out for them by their parents. You, the godparent, may have a useful role in encouraging parents to allow their children to develop as their own people, rather than fit the parental model. It could be that a sensitive card or gift from you received on the day a godchild has not succeeded or fulfilled expectations will mean more to your godchild than anything you could give on a day of great achievement, such as when they pass ten 'A' levels or win the marathon. What must be communicated is that the godchild is loved and valued, full stop. A person's value is not conditional on their achievements.

It is also worth remembering that life is not made up of special days and high points. Most of the time is much more average. A phone call, e-mail or other communication from a godparent can help a godchild feel special on average days too. And it works the other way round, as well.

'Sharing – unexpected phone calls when they just ring up to tell you something good or bad.'

'I receive a welcome telephone call if there is any special news.'

It is great *'being put on a child's holiday postcard list because I am "special" to them.'*

Sad Days

In looking at special days, when things are going well, we noted that not all days are like that. Most are average. Some are really hard and painful. This will certainly be true for your godchild, just as it is for anyone else. A child may experience:

- ○ failures
- ○ illness or accident – their own, or that of someone close to them
- ○ loss of a pet, a grandparent, a parent, brother or sister, or a close friend, and the accompanying grief and bereavement
- ○ breakdown in their own relationships with school friends, boy- or girlfriends, partners, and parents
- ○ family disruption or breakdown when parents split up or divorce.

As hinted earlier, the home, which should have provided a safe and nurturing environment, may have been for them a place of dispute, oppression, pain, domestic violence or abuse.

Again, the godparent's role of just 'being there' can be very important at such times. In the response to our questionnaire it was interesting that it was in this aspect of their role that many godparents felt they had experiences they wanted to share. After all the hope and promise of the baptism day, godparents who had managed over the months and years to build a strong and meaningful relationship with their godchild spoke of how they had shared more difficult times. But let the godparents speak for themselves:

'I have "been there".'

'I have maintained relationships, particularly during teen and early adult years. I have been available as they have needed/wanted to share – even if they needed someone to scream at.'

'I remember supporting the family and my godchildren through several crises.'

'I supported some of them through major loss (of a parent and of friends).'

'Sadly her mother died from cancer, aged 63, a devastating blow. After the funeral and return to our normal lives, I was always available by telephone to listen and hopefully advise, talking about the one we both loved and missed so much. I sent her a book which comforted me and which I hoped in time would help her. When recently her father married again I listened and understood the pain.'

'...the support I felt able to contribute at the time of the death of their mother.'

Of course, one of the traditionally received understandings of the role of the godparent was to 'be there *in extremis*' and maybe to take over the role of a parent or parents who died. Godparents responding to our questionnaire wrote of a preparedness *'to be responsible for the child if a crisis occurs'*; *'to be a substitute parent if there is no immediate family if the parents die'*; *'should the need arise, to act* in loco parentis*'*; to be *'guardians or close supporters if the child's parents died or were ill or incapacitated'*.

Sometimes even today parents die while the children are relatively young, though this does not automatically mean that a godparent is expected to take over as guardian, and in most cases this will not happen. Many more parents separate and divorce, sometimes with little acrimony but often with a great deal. The evidence suggests that dispute between parents followed by separation and/or divorce can cause long-term difficulties for the children. They need as much stability and continuity as possible. It seems that this is a situation where godparents have much to offer, and often do offer it.

The report of a Working Party of the Board for Social Responsibility of the Church of England, *Something to Celebrate: Valuing Families in Church and Society*, contained (on page 173) practical advice in a simple five-point guide which godparents may find helpful:

'It will greatly assist the family if they can be helped to

○ tell their children a coherent story of what has happened and why;

○ maintain relationships with both "sides" of the wider family;

○ grieve for what is lost and cannot be restored;

○ hold on to and treasure what was good and of value in their past relationship;

○ approach the future realistically in terms of the inevitable changes in lifestyle, social life and financial provision.'

Godparents wrote:

'Two of my godchildren had parents who eventually split up – these children have always holidayed with us and I am much closer to them because they needed more support. The 24-year-old still spends a lot of time with us and considers it his second home. These are practical things but I feel we were able to give them stability and a safe environment.'

'When the marriage of a goddaughter's parents broke up, finding a very special "family" role and providing continuity, stability and support.'

'I took my godson to his father's second wedding, picking him up from his mother's house. He was five. On the way back he asked me quite simply – who do you prefer, mummy or daddy? This was both very sad but also precious that he could ask me because I knew both his parents.'

'Coping with the aftermath of an acrimonious divorce. It is painful to realise that my godson no longer has contact with his father.'

'When there is family rupture, the breakdown of relationships, etc., the godparent's role can be important and challenging. Not taking sides with a parent, supporting the children and helping them to know themselves still loved, supporting them in

making hard choices – all takes sensitivity ... Sometimes the godparent can be involved in trying to work out "best solutions" for children, working with both parents who may find it hard to communicate.'

'If parents separate, make sure you are there for the child and perhaps to help the parents work out how parenting can be achieved by both after the separation.'

Of course, the breakdown may not be in the relationship between parents but in the relationship between child and parent:

'One godchild married against her parents' wishes and there was a major family breakdown between her and both parents. During this time I became surrogate mother – even receiving cards on Mother's Day – and eventually some reconciliation was achieved. I really did very little but hope that "being there" was an anchor.'

It is also worth noting from some of the godparents' stories that the support and love is not all in one direction. Godparents are both givers and receivers.

'There have been times when some have experienced trauma – illness, relationship breakdown, death of a parent – and my role has been/is to be there for them, alongside listening, crying, praying, supporting and being practical, such as caring for siblings while parents are at hospital with a sick child. When I have had difficulties they have been there for me too – supporting emotionally and practically.'

'When I was in hospital three years ago, she visited me a number of times at great inconvenience to herself and on one of those occasions she took my hand and said I looked at her just as her mother used to. This was "special".'

'My eldest godson was a great support on the day of my husband's funeral, escorting me to a front pew (in the absence of any children of our own) and generally acting as a son might.'

Clearly, for some people the relationship between godparent and godchild, though painful, becomes very significant.

Days of Decision

Many godparents said they had tried to become someone their godchild would feel able to talk things over with:

'Be there if they want to talk about any problems as they get older, especially around the teenage years.'

You may be invited to share conversations over decisions to be made, minor or major:

'An 18-year-old asked my advice about after-shave. Holding two, he asked me to smell them and suggest which might be the more appropriate and pleasant fragrance to wear to an important party.'

'Adult to adult with my grown-up goddaughter – seeing the sights of London, and talking future career plans – hers, over a lunch.'

As a godparent, you can be to your godchild an alternative adult, someone safe with the parental seal of approval, but at the same time independent and objective. You may, therefore, be approached to talk about things on which your godchild and a parent disagree, or something that your godchild is uncertain about – either in terms of a personal decision or in terms of how to approach the issue when telling parent(s). Examples might be whether to:

○ leave school and start work, or stay on and go to university

○ leave home

○ work abroad

○ choose a partner, especially if the partner is of the same sex and your godchild has a parent who is uncertain about or actively hostile towards lesbians and gays

○ get married or not

○ have children or not.

'You are there to be "an ear" if the older child finds it hard to talk to the parents.'

'You are somebody the child could talk to apart from their parents, especially if they feel uncomfortable to talk to them about certain issues.'

'When an 18-year-old phoned to talk about leaving home – how could she best help her parents to let her go because they were struggling and she recognised this.'

Even general conversations with a godchild, that may not be about making a decision at the time, may prepare your godchild for important future decisions and may provide a significant part of the foundation on which good decisions are made.

'We talked for 45 minutes on our own about women we admired and why, how to deal with people we don't like, what kind of people we want to be like.'

Of course, in the end any decision your godchildren make must be their own. It may well be that one of the reasons they have chosen to talk to you is that they feel parental pressure to make particular decisions that go against what they see as the best or the right choices. As a godparent, it is a good idea to affirm that you appreciate being part of such a conversation, you trust them to make a good decision, and you will respect their decision when it has been made, whether or not you agree with it!

You may become involved in explaining the decision to a parent, especially if they are strongly opposed to it, or think their child is being stupid or obstinate and that you are being irresponsible in taking a different line.

And what if you disagree with your godchild's decision and it later turns out that you were probably right? Obviously this is no time for gloating, and sympathy is more appropriate. Affirm that we all make mistakes from time to time and, indeed, that is how we learn. Not all decisions are simple choices between two alternatives, one of which is obviously right and the other wrong. Very few decisions are that simple. A choice made between two equally convincing alternatives may be no more right at the time than would the alternative choice, but it may become right or wrong as it is acted upon.

Whether the decision was right or wrong in your eyes from the start, whether or not it worked out, your main responsibility as a godparent is as it was before – to 'be there'.

Days on a Faith Journey

We have already seen that the traditional understanding of the godparent role is by prayer, example and teaching to help bring the godchild up in the Christian faith so that in due time s/he will confirm the promises made by godparents and parents at the baptism. However, in a society where churchgoing is no longer the 'norm', confirmation is no longer a 'rite of passage' for the majority of young people. Many people have no faith commitment. Some young people are cautious about committing themselves to anything that reeks of establishment. Even young people who take Christianity very seriously often do so in a much more questioning and less traditional way than previous generations seem to have done. So, however committed the godparent and however cooperative the parent, young people will make their own decisions about whether or not to be confirmed. Sharing together about questions of faith is probably far less one-way than the traditional model envisaged. This certainly seems to have been the experience of many of the godparents who contacted us.

Some were very clear that a major part of their role was to do with the development of their godchild's faith and spiritual awareness. They spoke of *'encouragement of spiritual awareness'*, the responsibility *'to help and guide in their spiritual search'*, *'to be a spiritual guide'*, a *'nurturer of Christian/faith development'*. Another *'had long discussions in the early days about Christianity and its relevance to our lives'*.

One was very specific and saw the role as *'to ensure that the gospel is clearly presented to the child during their youth and a decision elicited.'*

Some were obviously concerned that their godchildren had not taken the next step towards church membership and faith commitment:

'Knowing that my teenage godchild hadn't made a decision for Christ, I travelled to see her, took her to the best coffee house in town, and talked to her about my faith and God's challenge in her life.'

'Don't give the impression that because they no longer go to Sunday School, because of various reasons … you have lost interest in them.'

Another had *'made it possible for some of them to attend camps, events and festivals organised and run by Christians.'*

Some reported that their godchild's step towards Christian commitment was a major highlight in their relationship:

'I felt privileged to see him formally baptised as an 11-year-old (he was dedicated as a baby).'

'I appreciated attending his confirmation service, which was full of hope. Somehow it reminded me of God's care for him and future plans for him.'

'When she made a personal commitment to Jesus Christ whilst we were taking part in a service at the Albert Hall during an MAYC (Methodist Association of Youth Clubs) weekend, it really was a very precious moment for both of us.'

As the children got older, whether confirmed or not, some godparents saw the faith side of their responsibility as a major (and exciting) ongoing challenge. Others felt their responsibilities were coming to an end, especially if it was hard to maintain contact.

'Especially now that my eldest goddaughter is in her teens and has just been confirmed, it has been fun exploring the questions of faith with her.'

'Once the godchild is confirmed the particular contact is less strong, and depends on the relationship with the rest of the family and the ease of communication.'

Several godparents described the difficulty of sharing faith with their godchildren if the parents were not Christian. The importance of discussing parental expectations when a person is being asked to be a godparent is clear.

One godparent, reflecting on how her understanding of her role had changed over the years, wrote:

'My understandings of the Good News, human development and life in general have changed and informed my understanding of the role of godparent. I am more

relaxed in the role, have a more holistic view of the role and of children – I see God in them. I have a greater understanding of how faith might grow and see myself as significant in their lives but only part of it. They "read" me and other people, they interact with the world God has made and make their connections. They want to know my story, their story and his story and how they connect. In the end they make their choices and I do not have to be prescriptive in that – merely "let them" by supporting and encouraging. In short, I live with a different set of images. I am travelling with them, learning and growing alongside.'

Sharing the journey was a recurring theme, as the relationship between godparent and godchild matured. One godparent appreciated *'their questions, which have sometimes been very challenging to me and caused me to think and grow.'* Another was moved that her goddaughter *'assures me of her prayers for me since I was widowed just two years ago.'*

In Conclusion

In good times or bad, when there is a difficult decision to be made, news to be shared, something to discuss – whether faith, life, love, work, education or aftershave – godparents who manage to sustain the relationship with their godchild over the years have obviously found it to be very rewarding.

In 1945, Robert Graves was invited to become the godfather of a friend's child. He said:

'I think the godfather's job in this modern world is always to be the chap to whom the godchild writes if he or she has got into a real jam and needs to be bailed out, or fished out of a stew; and with whom he/she goes to stay, uninvited, at times of emotional crisis.'

Broken Images: Selected Letters of Robert Graves, 1914-1946,
Hutchinson, 1982.

We might not use the word 'chap' as comfortably as Robert Graves. We might say it in different words, as did some of the godparents who wrote to us:

'You are there to lend a listening ear if times are difficult.'

'It's about being a sounding board whenever she's needed it.'

The words are different but the sentiment and the experience are the same, as some of the stories shared in this chapter have shown.

Chapter 5
Godparent Support
A chapter for godparents

Most people receiving an invitation to become a godparent describe it as an affirming experience. Friends or family members have actually asked you to share with them the Christian upbringing of their precious child. Could they have bestowed a greater honour on you?

The role of godparent is an important one as you will be aware, especially if you read Chapters 2 and 6 of this book. Most people know that it will involve a baptism service, the making of promises, a party and probably the buying of a gift for the godchild. You may be briefed so that you know what to expect on the baptism day. The day comes, you find it a meaningful and fun experience – but what then?

Obviously you want to do your best for your new godchild but this may be a new role for you. You may feel the need of support and there is some available. Some you can provide for yourself, rather as you might ensure that you are well nourished by eating a balanced diet. Other support for you in fulfilling your godparent role may come from other people. Let us begin by considering self-support.

Self-Support

There are three areas for self-support that might be considered. Firstly, be natural and sincere about building up your own spiritual life. Be as creative and supportive of yourself as you can. Allow yourself time to be quiet, to reflect, to pray, to worship, to do what feeds your own spirit.

Secondly, consider the spiritual development of your godchild. Many godparents have had little opportunity to think about children's spirituality and their development in faith. Those who do this not only gain insight into children and their growth but find their personal understanding enhanced too. So be imaginative in encouraging your godchild.

Thirdly, make a list of the times in the year when you intend to meet or have other contact with your godchild. Make sure these and other special days or dates are recorded in your diary or written on the calendar so that they will not be forgotten. Ensure that the child's name is added to your Christmas list and that the birthday date is written in large letters so that it is remembered. Regular ongoing contact and remembering of your godchild will be important for you as well as the child.

Co-godparent Support

You are not alone. You will share the responsibility for the Christian nurture of your godchild with other godparents, usually two. The parents have brought you together with others, perhaps from different fields or periods of their own lives. One of you may be a particular friend of the mother, perhaps a college friend or colleague, while another may be a long-term friend of the father. It may be that you do not know each other well. Indeed you may meet for the first time at the baptism. Now you have an opportunity of forming a friendship group that might meet at regular family events. You might arrange to keep in touch and to co-operate to ensure that at least one of you is present at events that are important to your godchild, such as a football or netball match, so that s/he feels supported. This is especially important if the three of you live busy lives and live at some distance from your godchild. So before leaving the baptism party make sure that you have the names, addresses, telephone numbers and possibly e-mail addresses of your co-godparents. Do what you can to become a team, recognising that you have particular gifts and strengths that will be useful in supporting your godchild and that your co-godparents may have others. Together you can ensure that your godchild is well supported.

You, and your co-godparents, will find it helpful if you do develop the concept of the 'godparent team', with one doing what another cannot and one being a particular support to your godchild at a period when the others cannot be so easily available. More than this, however, together you can provide a richness by virtue of the fact that you complement each other, all having a part to play in the Christian nurture of your godchild. Being one of three godparents therefore does not mean duplication; rather the more synergy and overlap there is between godparents, the more the godchild will benefit.

Support from the Worshipping Community

The church can assist you in your personal growth and as a godparent by devising ways of valuing you and other godparents. Find out what your church does so that you can benefit from, say, a group considering children's faith development or family support, or a godparents' group. Such a group may helpfully discuss ideas for supporting children, or theological issues like your godchild receiving Holy Communion prior to confirmation. If nothing is happening and you feel the need of something, then talk to the church leadership and discuss the possibilities of the church doing something. A church can also pray for godparents and their godchildren. If there is anything in particular that you would value the church including in its intercessions then make your needs known. Church members cannot pray intelligently if they do not have the relevant details. If, however, the matter to be prayed about is of a private or sensitive nature, it may be appropriate to invite one or two church members to join you in prayer and to respect the confidence you have placed in them. Remember: if a church takes no interest in godparents or sponsors it is hard to see how they can be expected to take a high interest in their godchildren – the congregation makes promises alongside the godparents of every child baptised in the church.

Support through Published Resources

M any churches have a bookstall that includes a range of published resources. The person responsible for the bookstall will no doubt have catalogues from various publishers that you may be able to explore before ordering specific resources for yourself or your godchild. If not, then denominational children's officers or youth officers will have some knowledge of what is available and so will Christian bookshops or the person responsible for the 'religion' section of a major bookshop. Often denominational staff hold inspection copies of key publications. Some books, audio cassettes and videos may be helpful to you, while others may be shared with your godchild or given as a gift. Sometimes presentation sessions may be hosted to inform church members of what is available. At these sessions the contents, rationale and quality of resources may be explained and discussed so that you can choose your resources from an informed position.

Support from the Godchild's Parents

P arents are central to the spiritual development of their children. The home is the microcosm of the church, sometimes described as the church in the home, for the growing child. It is essential, therefore, that you co-operate with them in nurturing their children. For this to happen they must provide you with access to their children and you must be careful not to exclude them consciously or unconsciously from your activities with the child. You are part of your godchild's extended family and are not just your role as godparent. Keep in touch with parents as well as the child. Parents can help their child to stay in touch with you and keep you in touch with family life and with your godchild's progress. They and you can do everything possible to link your godchild with the local church community, its all-age worship and service as well as its age-appropriate children's and youth activities. Then your godchild may become an integrated member of the local Christian community and be further supported in his or her growth towards greater spiritual maturity.

Never Alone

So you are not alone in fulfilling your role as godparent. In the baptism service you probably made promises with the words: 'With God's help I/we will.' It is important to believe that God will help you and to see that part of that help may be found through the support of others with whom you share the task – parents, other godparents, the local church (yours and the child's), and those who publish resources. It is also worth remembering and taking heart from the fact that you have been chosen for this role because others perceive that you can and will do it.

Chapter 6
Godparents and
the Local Church

A chapter for all church people

This chapter is mainly for members, officers and ministers of local churches, to encourage you to consider how you relate to godparents and, in doing so, to reflect on your church's policy and practice towards parents and young children. Over the years, different denominations have produced resources to help local churches develop their policy and practice but, in the end, it is up to the local church to make sure that they have a policy and that they offer a welcome to parents, godparents and young children alike.

The Initial Approach

When parents want their baby to be baptised, whom do they approach and how are they received? Is it the minister's job, or are there one or more members of the church whose specific role is to meet, visit, talk with and prepare parents for their child's baptism?

Whoever talks to parents, when an initial approach has been made, there are various important matters to be sorted out:

○ Basic details – names, addresses, dates, and so on

○ Why do the parents want their baby baptised? What are their church links and how do they understand baptism? Is baptism appropriate or would it be better to arrange a thanksgiving, dedication or other service?

○ Do the parents know what takes place in your church, and how do they understand it in terms of a child's way of entry into the Christian community? What does this mean for their own involvement in the life of the church?

○ What about godparents? Earlier in this book we suggested that godparents have probably already been chosen and invited by the time parents approach the church. Whether they have or not, it is important for the representative from the church to explore with parents the role of godparents and the promises they will be asked to make. The discussion might also explore the expectations that parents have of godparents, and how the parents envisage they will enable the godparents to keep the promises they are asking them to make.

○ How does baptism fit into the rest of the life of your church? In what ways does the church offer support to parents and young children? For example, is there a crèche, a regular pram service, a toddlers' group, children's activities and events, all-age worship, communion services where children are welcome, parenting groups and courses, pastoral support or visits?

At a first meeting it can be helpful to provide some material for parents to take away and look at, including details of your church and its life, a copy of the baptism service, and/or a copy of this or some other appropriate book for them or the potential godparents.

In the Methodist baptism service, after the parents and godparents have made their promises, *the whole congregation* is asked to respond to a question: 'Members of the body of Christ, we rejoice that these children have been baptised. Will you so maintain the Church's life of worship and service that they may grow in grace and the knowledge and love of God and of his son Jesus Christ our Lord?' They reply, 'With God's help we will.'

The United Reformed Church has a similar question: 'Do you, as members of Christ's body and trusting in God's grace, promise to pray for A..., provide for the teaching of the gospel, and live a Christian life in the family of God?'

The baptism service in the Church of England's *Alternative Service Book* has the congregation joining in an acclamation of welcome.

Whether the words are of promise or of welcome, they signify that all the members of the church have a responsibility towards children who are brought for baptism. It is not just up to the parents, godparents, minister or children's workers in the church. Baptised children are everyone's responsibility. That is why it is important for each local church to have a clear policy about baptism and the pastoral care of parents and young children.

Being Welcoming to Godparents

When the names of any godparents have been decided and notified to the representative of the church responsible for making baptism arrangements, the church could contact the godparents either directly or via the parents, to offer them a welcome and help them prepare for their important role. It would be possible to send them a booklet, such as the one you are reading now, or a leaflet about what it means to be a godparent. Some churches use a professionally produced one, such as *Becoming a Godparent: a guide for godparents and parents.* Others produce their own. This example comes from Manor Road Methodist Church, Whetstone, London N20:

What It Means To Be A Godparent

If you have been asked to be a godparent at a baptism this information has been written to help you understand what is involved and what is expected of you.

Being a godparent is a privilege and a joy. It is a sign of the trust the family has in you. Often parents choose friends. You may also find you have been chosen because you are to be a legal guardian of the child. As a godparent, it is appropriate to buy a small gift like a book or video of Christian stories, or a child's Bible, for your godchild.

Godparents are expected to support the parents and to encourage the child to understand the Christian belief in God. You are expected to be an example to the child in the way that you live your life, that is, with care and love and respect for the world and other people. You are expected to make the promise printed below. You will be asked to stand with the family at the front of the church to make the promise.

The promise is a reply to the question: Will you help these parents to nurture their child in the Christian faith?

Answer: With God's help we will.

If you find that you cannot make the promise, then you can offer to be a 'supporter' of the child and family, rather than a godparent. You can stand alongside the parents and godparents but not say something that you do not believe. Supporters and godparents are welcome in our church. (If a family would like their child to be baptised, but do not think they have anyone to make the promise as a godparent, a member of our church will make the promise and be a church godparent.)

It is important to consider how godparents can be prepared for their part in the baptism service. When do they need to be there? Where and with whom do they sit? When and where do they stand? What words do they say? Are there particular things they are expected to do, like holding a candle or the baby, at some point? The more easy the godparents feel about their part in the service, the better the service will go and the more it is likely to mean to them and to everyone else. The necessary information can be conveyed in a letter or leaflet, at a rehearsal, or – and this is really a bit too late – before the service, on the day itself.

Those responsible for the baptism service in the church can ensure that the part played by godparents is recognised. Their presence can be acknowledged and they can be welcomed. Their role can be mentioned or described as part of a short address. They can be included in any formal photographs. Some churches give them a 'thank you' card on the day, signed by the minister and with thanks 'for promising your support in the Christian upbringing' of the child. SPCK produces a card *For a Godparent*. Inside is an outline of the duties of godparents, and 'a greeting and a blessing' for the godparent, signed by the minister who has taken the baptism service.

The Baptism Service: Points in Preparation

A lot of different things are happening when there is a baptism.

The church is welcoming a new member of the Christian community – in the traditional way. Generation after generation has been welcomed in a similar way for two thousand years and other new members will continue to be welcomed into the Christian community across the world. The child joins millions of others who have been and are part of God's family, the Church.

The child's family and friends are marking an important moment in the child's life and their own. It is a day for a special family get-together and the service will probably be followed by some sort of celebration, a meal or a party. Different generations may have travelled many miles to be part of this day. The people who have gathered may not do so very often – perhaps only for baptisms, weddings and funerals. Some (and maybe most) of those who gather may not be used to going to church. They may find the whole occasion rather strange and perhaps embarrassing. They may be worried about getting things right, or they may not take the service very seriously and just look forward to it being over so they can get on with the party.

Members of the church's regular congregation probably have mixed views about this baptism, although, in churches where there are many baptisms, they take place at a separate time so the normal congregation is not present. If the baptism takes place as part of a normal service, some members of the congregation will be pleased to see new people in church, but sad that they do not see these same people on other weeks, especially if they live locally. Some may be asking themselves how seriously the parents and godparents are taking their promises, particularly in relation to the Christian upbringing of the child: 'We haven't seen these people since they were here for the baptism of their older child, two and a half years ago. People shouldn't make promises unless they mean to keep them!'

It is because of concerns such as these that some churches have quite strict baptismal policies and will only baptise children where there is some likelihood and evidence of ongoing involvement in the life of the church on the part of parents. Others take the view that the baptism helps the child and family to mark a significant point of change in their lives when they often feel closer to God or recognise their need of his blessing even if they are not regular church-goers. Those who take the latter view sometimes see the baptism family and godparents as giving the church an opportunity to join in caring for the child. How many congregations take up this opportunity and develop relationships in an ongoing way?

However strict or otherwise a particular church's baptism policy, baptisms are occasions when at least some of the family and friends who gather are likely to be people who do not usually go to church. That being so, it is worth asking what can be done to help people feel 'at home' in these strange surroundings. Here are some questions that might help:

○ What kind of welcome is offered at the door of the church, as people arrive?

○ Are members of the baptism party shown where to sit or are they expected to guess?

○ Are things said to make it clear that it is good to see everyone there, or are visitors left feeling they have disturbed other people's slumbers?

○ If people are expected to find the order of service in a large and complicated book, are clear instructions given to help them do so? Or is the baptism service printed in a separate book or on a card?

○ Do they have to find their way through a whole pile of different books to discover the words for hymns and songs?

○ Is it clear when people are supposed to stand, sit or move?

○ If there is a collection, is good warning given?

○ Is the whole occasion one that will make people want to come again, or will they simply be relieved that it is over?

The conviction of the writers of this book is that a baptism can and should offer people a good experience of the church community. It should also be an occasion that makes clear what baptism is about and does something to offer support to parents and godparents, who have ongoing responsibilities towards the child being baptised.

Being a Child-friendly Church

In the previous section we considered briefly how people who do not attend church regularly might be helped to feel welcome when they come to a baptism service. This leads naturally on to the question of how 'child-friendly' is your church? If the person to be baptised is a baby, s/he is unlikely to notice the finer details, but there are often other children present at a baptism. And the parents and godparents of children being baptised will very quickly get a feel for how your church welcomes children.

It may be that on the day of the baptism everyone present goes out of their way to smile at the baby and its escorts. But what if a parent brings the same baby back to the same church the week after? And what if the baby makes a noise or, worse, a smell at an inconvenient moment? Some parents clearly feel embarrassed at the thought of coming back to church with a young baby. Where will they feed it? Where will they change it? What do they do if it cries?

Quite a lot of churches now have facilities for changing babies' nappies but they are not always easy to find! Some have special places for parents to take their young children if they are noisy or hungry. Other churches are quite happy for the parent to stay where they are with their child. Yet others have members who will go and sit with parents with young children, so they do not feel so much 'on show' and also to share the care.

As children get older, the kinds of noises they make during services change. Some bring noisy toys, or enjoy the sound of dropping hymn books or collection money on the floor. Others clearly get bored and tell their parents so in very loud whispers. Some churches now provide bags with soft toys, books, paper and equipment for drawing etc. These are perhaps hung on hooks clearly visible in the entrance area, so a child or parent can ask for one as they go into church. Such provision both offers something interesting but quieter to occupy children and makes a clear statement that children are welcome in this church.

There are other ways that a church building and the worship that takes place in it can be made user-friendly for children. Is there somewhere they can reach to hang their coats when they arrive? Are there interesting things to look at, touch, explore? When something important is going on in a service, such as when a baby is baptised or when bread is broken and wine shared, are the children able to see what is going on? Does everything that takes place depend on a reading age that would enable you to read the Guardian or are some parts of what goes on suitable for people, of whatever age, who cannot read well? Is the music all slow and Victorian? When coffee is provided at the end of the service is there also something for children?

Churches have different ways of providing for children of various ages. Some, particularly smaller ones, make no specific provision because they rarely see children, but it is still worth thinking about children who may be present as visitors. Others have a whole range of provision, from crèches for the very young to Sunday School or Junior Church and young people's groups. Some churches involve children and young people in worship in all kinds of ways, including drama, music groups or choirs, and sharing bread and wine at Communion. However it is done, it is important to find ways to give clear signals that all are welcome here, whatever your age, stage of faith, background, or status.

For parents whose children are baptised in the church, there may be things to see which link their child with all the others who have been baptised in the church over the years. Somewhere there will be a baptismal register, and when a child grows a little older it is good to be able to show them their name in the register. Some churches display cradle rolls or 'First Steps' rolls on the wall, with the names of children received into the church community. Again, as a child starts to learn to read, it is good to be able to show them their name on the roll. There are churches where the names and photos of children who have been baptised recently are displayed on a notice board – so that they can be recognised by members of the congregation and also to serve as a reminder to pray for the child and family.

Helping to create a child-friendly church is the responsibility of all the members of the church. Obviously the decision-makers and the money-spenders have particular responsibilities. But, perhaps above all, to get this right it is important to ask children and their parents for their views. What ideas do they have? What would they like to see done?

Arranging Reasonable Godparent Care

Having considered how a church caters for people in general, and children and their parents in particular, we need to ask how a church caters for the needs of godparents.

Earlier in this chapter we described how some churches provide leaflets or other materials for people who have been invited to be the godparents of children to be baptised in that church. Providing such a leaflet both gives useful information and advice to potential godparents and says that you treat godparents as important people – important enough to have thought about what you can do to help them as they become godparents.

We also suggested that there are ways to help godparents on the day of the baptism itself, and noted that some churches provide 'thank you' cards or other tokens for godparents to take away with them as souvenirs of the occasion and reminders of their responsibilities. These things can be appreciated. One godparent wrote: *'I was given a card by some of the churches with a godparenting promise; along with photos, these are helpful aides-mémoire to prayer – and making a phone call! They are on the pelmet in the study where I see them frequently.'*

Some churches follow up baptisms with annual 'cradle roll' or 'First Steps' services, where all the children, parents and godparents involved in baptisms over the past year are invited back for a special service. Others mark the anniversaries of baptisms by sending a card to the child and maybe to the family. This can be extended to godparents – a card can remind them that a year ago they were godparents at the baptism and include the church's good wishes and hope that they are finding the role rewarding.

Here are some other possible ideas for supporting godparents:

○ Church bookstalls and libraries could contain resources for godparents – books, leaflets, cards, advice on presents for godchildren.

○ From time to time there could be a discussion group for godparents, or other groups could take godparenting as a theme and invite people to share their experiences of being godparents or being godparented. Such a session can be particularly useful for coming up with new ideas.

○ Things said at baptism services to encourage new godparents can also be a source of fresh encouragement to those who are existing godparents, as can special prayers for godparents on other occasions.

○ An annual service or moment of rededication.

In later years, there are ways in which churches can encourage children to talk about and strengthen their links with godparents. An obvious moment when the godparent relationship is important is confirmation, when some churches make a point of encouraging confirmation candidates to contact/invite their godparents to the service.

Godparents are asked to make a commitment in the context of a formal public service in church. Our hope is that they will take that commitment seriously – and this book has tried to explore some of the implications of doing so. But, if godparents are to take the role seriously, the church needs to do the same.

Constructively Reviewing Your Approach on a Regular Basis

This chapter has been aimed at members, officers and ministers of local churches. Through it we hope to encourage you to look at where baptisms fit into the wider life of your church and to explore ways in which your approach to baptisms may affect what kind of community you are. We have encouraged you to consider how children and their parents and godparents will feel welcome in your church.

Our hope is that the rest of this book will have given you some pause for thought, and may lead to some discussion and action in your church. We also hope that you will involve other people in your discussions, especially children, parents and godparents. They will be able to tell you how they have experienced your church. They may also have some good ideas on changes that might be made.

Things change and so do people. Whatever changes you do or do not make now, it is important to revisit these issues from time to time to see how things are going and whether other changes are needed.

Chapter 7
Where did the Idea of
Godparents Come From?
Some background

Understandings of Baptism

A brightly coloured card arrived through the post announcing *Joy Story 2: to infancy and beyond*. It announced the birth of a second child, a daughter, and included an invitation to her 'Landing Party', her parents' title for the celebration of God's gift to them of a daughter. Despite its unusual name, the celebration will follow some of the traditions of the Christian denomination to which the parents belong. There will be those present who pray for the child and who will make promises to be significant in her life as her godparents or sponsors. They will make their promises publicly and begin, or perhaps continue, a relationship with their godchild that may be sustained throughout their lives.

It may be that you, the reader, are a godparent or that you have godparents. Have you ever stopped to think where the idea of godparents came from? Are you aware of the different approaches to baptism that different Christian denominations take? In this chapter we will attempt to address these questions. Firstly, however, let's take a few moments to consider baptism, the event at which so many godparents make their promises to support their godchild and family. What is baptism all about?

Turning to the New Testament, there are five quotations that might help to anchor our thinking about baptism. Each is concerned with 'newness'.

A new commitment

'...Jesus came from Nazareth of Galilee, and was baptised by John in the Jordan' (Mark 1.9, *New Revised Standard Version*). Remember the event: the fiery John foretelling the coming of the expected Messiah who would save his people, and calling them to repentance. Their baptism in the River Jordan was a sign of their turning from the past and committing themselves to a future with God. Then came Jesus, who fully associated with them in baptism, and the wonderful words from God, the Father: 'This is my Son, the Beloved, with whom I am well pleased' (Matthew 3.17, *NRSV*).

A new identity

The sacramental nature of the act of baptism in the Church is described in Romans 6.4: 'By our baptism, then, we were buried with him and shared his death, in order that, just as Christ was raised from death by the glorious power of the Father, so also we might live a new life' (*Good News Bible*). Compare this with Colossians 2.12: Paul, writing to the church in Rome, describes the mystery of baptism which brings the baptised believer into union with Christ and gives him or her a new identity as a child of God with a new life lived under God's grace.

A new experience

'He saved us, not because of any works of righteousness that we had done, but according to his mercy, through the water of rebirth and renewal by the Holy Spirit' (Titus 3.5, *NRSV*). Baptism by water is a sign of washing or cleansing and is followed or accompanied by the experience of nourishment and renewal by the Holy Spirit.

A new membership

'For in the one Spirit we were all baptised into one body – Jews or Greeks, slaves or free...' (1 Corinthians 12.13, *NRSV*). Here baptism is seen as a sign of membership of a cross-cultural, cross-status, transnational community of believers referred to as 'a holy nation' in 1 Peter 2.9. Through baptism, then, we become members of the Church worldwide that transcends time – so baptism is a sign of Christian inclusiveness and solidarity or togetherness.

A new task

'Go therefore and make disciples of all nations, baptising them in the name of the Father and of the Son and of the Holy Spirit, and teaching them to obey everything that I have commanded you' (Matthew 28.19-20a, *NRSV*). The great commission, as this verse is known, makes clear the task of Christians which includes the baptising of new believers.

Reflecting on these verses and considering today's context, Christian baptism may be understood as:

○ Beginning a journey of faith (promising to turn 'from' and 'to')

○ Bearing the badge of Christ (receiving the sign of the Cross)

○ Believing in the riches of God's grace (accepting the washing of water)

○ Belonging to the family of God (feeling the welcome of others)

○ Becoming a light in God's world (taking the candle of witness)

It will be possible to find these components in any mainstream baptism service, a service that uses signs and symbols to enable us to engage with its mystery and meaning.

Christian baptism, in the name of God the Father, Son and Spirit, the Trinity, is recognised by the main Christian denominations. In other words, one main denomination will recognise the practice of another. It is not a sacrament to be repeated.

How Godparents Began

The notion of godparents emerged gradually out of the life and growth of the Christian Church. There are four 'stages' of that development that might help us to understand how godparenting began and developed.

○ **Early Church baptismal practice:** Candidates for baptism, called *catechumens,* were given a quite serious and lengthy period of training by teachers called catechists. Their baptism, by total immersion, took place on the eve of Easter Day so that they could participate fully in the Easter celebrations of the Eucharist, Lord's Supper or Holy Communion. The baptistery in a Byzantine church was a stone-built sunken bath with two sets of steps, one leading down into the water while another led up out of the water. Usually a recess was built for the priest administering the baptism to stand in and sometimes also a recess by each flight of steps for a deacon.

○ **The role of the sponsor for adults:** Adult candidates for baptism needed adult sponsors to help and support them in the baptism process. An adult sponsor was usually a mature Christian who had encouraged the candidate to prepare for baptism, possibly by personal witness or personal affirmation, and may have commended the candidate to the bishop or priest. At the baptism itself the adult sponsor acted as a character witness in the candidate's presentation to the bishop or priest, and helped by being ready to assist the newly baptised after immersion, e.g. by carrying spare clothes. On Easter Day, the day after baptism, the adult sponsor was alongside the newly baptised to introduce him or her to the congregation and to the Holy Communion. Afterwards adult sponsors were Christian companions offering encouragement to the newly baptised as they continued their new lives as baptised members of the church.

○ **The role of the sponsor in relation to households:** There were occasions when whole households were baptised. On such occasions the sponsor for the adults extended Christian friendship and support to the children of the family as well. Part of the sponsor's role was to assist the family by accompanying, guiding and even holding the children at the time of the baptism itself. Although attending primarily to the adult candidates, the sponsor was an example and encouragement to the children of a baptised household.

○ **The role of the sponsor of individual children:** Child baptism appears to have developed in the second century when the child's sponsor was concerned to see that the child of baptised parents was also presented for baptism. They were concerned for the child's salvation and for the spiritual solidarity of the family.

The sponsor of a child was invariably present at the child's baptism, which in Eastern practice continued to be by total immersion. Later, however, when infant baptism became the norm, a smaller receptacle or font was used. The baptism, the anointing of the child, and the first receiving of the bread and wine all took place in the same ceremony. The sponsor or godparent of a child was therefore in a uniquely personal and spiritual relationship to the child. The relationship was seen to be so close that the Emperor Justinian is said to have prohibited marriage between godparents and godchildren.

Until around the ninth century it would have been increasingly usual for the child's sponsor to be a parent. The sponsor was available as an example and encourager in the Christian life. Later it was thought that in some circumstances a close but more dispassionate person might be able to perform the function better than a natural parent. From about the ninth century, godparents were expected to be people other than the natural parents and while the recommendation was for one sponsor, if there were two, one was to be male and the other female.

Changing Emphases in the Practice of Child Baptism

Over the years the emphases regarding children have therefore changed. Four shifts in emphasis have been identified below.

○ In the earliest times prominence was given to the family, the child being affected by, and part of, the baptismal faith of his or her parents and family.

○ Later the emphasis passed from the family to the Church and to the importance of its ministry of baptism to the child.

○ Then came the Reformation and the assertion of the need for the person who had been baptised to give evidence of understanding of the implications of the baptismal promises. To accommodate this the role of godparents was heightened by the publication of a *Catechism* that they were to use in teaching their godchildren. At about the same time the adult baptism movement began.

○ Towards the end of the twentieth century, the baptism of infants was valued as a 'rite of passage', especially in societies where there were many faith traditions. Infant baptism demonstrates the faith tradition of the child and family and gives the child a spiritual identity.

Where did the Idea of Godparents Come From?

The shifts in emphasis over the past two millennia might inform a new four-part interpretation of the role of godparents for the new millennium.

○ Godparents supporting the family of the baptised child in his or her religious care.

○ Godparents representing the welcome and love of the Church, the household of faith, for the baptised child.

○ Godparents acting as personal enablers for the growing child or young person. Part of the enabling role will be to find resources that will support the godchild in his or her journey of faith, including the implications of faith for daily living.

○ Godparents offering encouragement and reasonable protection to the baptised child in owning and affirming their Christian identity as provided for under *The United Nations Convention on the Rights of the Child, 1989.*

At this stage it may be worth pausing to reflect on the role of godparents as just described. It is obvious that the role is a significant one to be undertaken responsibly. Yet in many churches, especially in developed societies, the godparent role may be seen as relatively formal and empty. However, the reality is that in contemporary society the demands are quite the reverse! In a developed and more complex world, the obligations of the godparent are fuller and heavier than before. This raises a dilemma. At a time when godparents may be looked to for a more distinctive contribution to a child's life, many godparents are less sure and less well-grounded in their faith than they were in past generations.

It is important that parents and godparents should not be discouraged by this situation. Instead they might consider the following and be encouraged.

○ **The good news:** A godparent cannot be expected to do everything, and is certainly not expected to be a religious professional.

○ **The positives:** There are 'parental' aspects to godparenting. A godparent is more than a friend, and more than a mentor. A godparent will be a para-family member who will stand by the godchild for life, praying and setting an example.

○ **The specifics:** The duties of a godparent in supporting a godchild may be divided into three:

● supporting the child in receiving family love and security;

● facilitating the child's welcome into, and experience of the life of, the Church;

● encouraging the child in putting the joy and purpose of faith into practice in daily life.

○ **The general element:** The godparent is expected to affirm and protect the godchild's Christian individuality and his or her spiritual and religious rights just as nurtural parents (birth, adoptive, step-parents) would affirm and protect the person-hood and family identity of their child.

If we put together the three 'specifics' and the 'general element' from this list, we find an interesting parallel. Essentially what is looked for in today's godparents is a synthesis of the four shifts in emphasis in godparenting over the last 2000 years, but it is helpful to keep in mind that Jesus' disciples were and are ordinary people. At heart, godparents are ordinary Christians, 'generalists' in the best sense. Godparents cannot be expected to be angels or experts. However, sometimes it may be that someone would be esp-ecially suitable for their 'family' skills, another might be suitable for their church involvement, and someone else might be suitable because s/he is a good example of Christian living (perhaps unconsciously). In an ideal situation, three such people would make an excellent godparenting trio. Of course the selection process may never prove as neat and easy as this, but the model does show that choosing god-parents with different contributions to make does give a rationale which may be helpful to the godchild in both the short and long term.

Different Traditions

Churches have different traditions regarding godparents. Some of these differences reflect the way various denominations understand what godparents are and the part they play. Others are more to do with how practice has changed and developed over the years in a particular local church. We start with different denominations, and look at four examples – Anglican, Roman Catholic, United Reformed and Methodist.

Anglican churches

In the Church of England and other Anglican churches (Church in Wales, Church of Ireland, Episcopal Church of Scotland) it is usual to have three godparents, two of the same sex as the child and one of the opposite sex, but to have one godfather and one godmother is sufficient. Parents may be godparents to their own children, provided that the child has at least one other godparent. The Church expects godparents to be baptised and confirmed, but the requirement of confirmation can be relaxed. It was important that the godparents had been baptised and confirmed because the 1662 *Book of Common Prayer* made it clear that the primary responsibility for the child's Christian upbringing rested with the godparents. The minister was to 'instruct the parents or guardians of an infant to be admitted to Holy Baptism that the same responsibilities rest on them as are in the service of Holy Baptism required of the godparents.' More recent services, such as that in the 1980 *Alternative Service Book*, make clear that the parents bear the main responsibility for their child's upbringing, with godparents supporting them or sharing their role.

Roman Catholic churches

In the Roman Catholic Church it is normal for a child being baptised to have two godparents or 'sponsors', one male and one female. The baptism leaflet from the Cathedral Parish of St Mary and St Helen in Brentwood describes the sponsor's role as 'a model or an example of Christian life to a young child as the child grows into adulthood. The role of a sponsor involves the sharing of the Faith and the development of a close relationship with the child.' The same leaflet says the requirements for sponsors are that 'they must have received the Sacraments of Initiation – Baptism, Holy Communion and Confirmation – in the Catholic Church. They must be old enough, usually at least sixteen years of age, to fulfil their responsibilities. Baptised Christians of other denominations may not serve as sponsors because they are not members of the Catholic Church into which the child is to be initiated. They may serve, however, as a Christian Witness and be so designated in the Baptismal Register.' Not all priests demand that the second sponsor be a Roman Catholic. It is worth noting that in recent years the Catholic Church has been promoting the baptism of adults, with sponsors, as the norm, from which infant baptism is derived, although the number of infant baptisms far outweighs those of adults. The role of sponsor/godparent is being enhanced, as some sort of faith-companion, to play a part at other times, especially in childhood and adolescence. In many ways this reflects the practice of earlier centuries, already described in this chapter.

United Reformed churches

The United Reformed Church makes no mention of godparents in its current leaflet for ministers and elders about baptism and thanksgiving. However, the service in the current service book includes a promise to be made by what are called 'sponsors'. The promise is: 'Do you promise, trusting in God's grace, to pray and care for A... and support his/her family as you are able?' Cards are available to be given to sponsors or godparents to mark the day and thank them for promising their support in the child's Christian upbringing. Local churches vary in their practice and parents are encouraged to discuss the matter with the minister when they request baptism for their child.

Methodist churches

Methodist churches introduced 'sponsors' in the 1970s, with the intention that at least one sponsor would be chosen by the parents and another by the church. The 1999 *Methodist Worship Book* dropped the title 'sponsor' and adopted the more commonly used term 'godparent'. In the service the parents and godparents stand together around the font and together answer a question affirming their faith. After the child has been baptised, the parents or godparents may be given a candle. There is a special promise for godparents, made after the baptism: 'Will you help these parents to nurture their children in the Christian faith? With God's help we will.'

Baptist and other churches

The differences in approach between different denominations and local churches do not just relate to the part played by godparents. Some churches, especially those within the Baptist tradition, put the emphasis on people being baptised when they are of an age to make their own decision about faith commitment. In these churches, parents are more likely to be offered a 'thanksgiving' or 'dedication' service for their young child as they become part of the Christian community and start out on their faith journey.

As well as differences between the denominations, some practices and traditions within a denomination may vary from church to church but they will be broadly similar. In some churches, especially those where there are a lot of baptisms, the service will be held at a special time, separate from the main worship of the day. In other churches, the baptism forms part of the main service of the day so family members and guests not used to Sunday services may need warning of what's in store!

Sometimes, Christian parents who attend churches which do practise infant baptism prefer to encourage their children to make up their own minds whether to be baptised when they are older, and request a service of thanksgiving or dedication. Similar services are sometimes offered to parents who are not regular churchgoers or who are uncertain about making a public affirmation of faith. Where the service is a thanksgiving or dedication rather than a baptism, parents still sometimes invite friends or relatives to be 'godparents' to support them on the day and afterwards in their child's Christian upbringing.

New Challenges in Modern Times

One of the traditional roles of godparents was to be there for the child if their parents died or for any other reason were unable to look after them. Today, however, godparents do not have legal responsibilities and do not become guardians of their godchildren unless this is specifically requested and declared, for example in the parents' will. In an age when many parents died while their children were still relatively young and when there was no organised welfare provision, godparents sometimes ended up taking on much greater responsibilities for their godchildren than they had either hoped or expected. Few are called on to do this today.

But life can still be very hard for today's children. Every year the children's charity NCH Action for Children publishes a *Factfile*, based mainly on official government statistics. Its edition for the year 2000 included some interesting but also some very uncomfortable reading. Out of twelve million children living in the UK, three million lived in a lone-parent family and over a million lived in a stepfamily. Four million lived in poverty. On an average day:

- ○ 300 families with children would be accepted as homeless
- ○ 400 children would experience their parents' divorce
- ○ 34 children would be excluded from education
- ○ 87 children would be put on a child protection register
- ○ 15 children would be adopted
- ○ 2,700 children would have an accident and go to hospital.

The twentieth century saw major changes in family life, with much greater diversity of family patterns and experience. Many children's parents separate or divorce while the children are still young. Others experience poverty, violence, bullying, neglect, substance abuse, racial or sexual abuse and so on. For all kinds of reasons, parents cannot or do not always continue to look after their children as they would wish. Grandparents may play an important role in children's lives, especially if they live nearby. But many live hundreds of miles away, and others have lost or been deprived of contact because of an acrimonious breakdown in the relationship between the child's parents.

Children need adults who care about them, both within and beyond their family. In a world where families go through many transitions and where children need stability and continuity, there may be special roles and new perspectives for godparents today. While the role of godparents may have changed, it is still very important – and may sometimes be crucial.

Alongside the changes already described, the twentieth century also saw a major decline in the numbers of people attending church in the United Kingdom. There are many reasons for this and many solutions have been suggested to reverse the decline. It is too soon to say what will happen in the twenty-first century, though it is worth remembering that things have been bad for the churches before – travel around the country and see the ruins of medieval monasteries! And while the number of Christians in the UK has gone down, the number of Christians worldwide continues to rise, in some countries very dramatically.

The decline in churchgoing in the UK means that baptism and confirmation are not 'rites of passage' for the majority of the population any more. Many children are not baptised, so many children do not have godparents. As they grow up, they may not think about what godparents are until they are asked by a friend to be one. This raises all kinds of questions. Can a person not brought up in the Christian faith be an effective godparent? Can someone successfully undertake the role of godparent when the child's parents are not committed to the Christian faith and may only be having their child baptised to please their churchgoing parents, or because they like the idea and it provides an opportunity for another party and some great photos? How do you support a child's growth in faith in a world that perhaps takes faith less seriously?

Godparents answering our questionnaire raised some of these concerns:

'I think most people in today's climate view it as a social occasion with purely social obligations.'

'It seems that these days the position of godparent has become purely social.'

'You have a "christening" because it's "nice" and the thing to do.'

(Interestingly, in 1998 the Government's *Supporting Families* consultation document promoted the idea of secular baby-naming ceremonies, conducted by registrars – who already conduct an increasing proportion of marriages. If this idea becomes popular it may mean that some parents who would currently approach a church requesting their child's baptism will opt for a secular ceremony instead.)

It may be that at a time when many people do not bother with a church baptism and others do not seem to take it seriously any more, we have an opportunity to take another look at what godparents are for and to re-invent the role. If we are aware that our society has changed, our churchgoing habits have changed and our understanding of the needs of children has developed, maybe there is an important new role for godparents? The writers of this book believe godparents have lots to offer!

Broadly Defining the Task

So, what is a godparent? One of the questions in our questionnaire was: 'What do you understand the role of a godparent to be?' We received all kinds of replies, some of which have been looked at in this book. Some godparents had a very clear view of their 'spiritual' role (see Chapter 2). Others talked in more general terms. A godparent's role is:

○ *'to befriend the child'*

○ *'to be a loving support and spiritual guide'*

○ *'to look to the welfare of the child'*

○ *'to provide general interest and support'*

○ *'to offer a listening ear to children as they mature'*

One summed it up in three words: *'prayer, friendship and example'*.

Others emphasised the relationship with the parents: *'to help and support the parents'*, to be *'supportive of parents'*.

Where did the Idea of Godparents Come From?

One godparent encapsulated her understanding of the task in these terms: *'to pray for her, to see her now and then, to send presents and, if appropriate, to be a source of help when she is an adult.'* Another saw it as being a *'mentor, confidante, introducer of new ways of being and thinking, having fun, being an alternative adult in children's lives ... to take an interest in the child's total development, with particular interest in the spiritual side.'*

'In short, godparenting is like "another parent" not living at home with you who you can go over to for holidays. A keen interest in developing and preparing them for a successful adulthood by relating day-to-day activities, encouraging and advising them should also be taken. Most importantly, an encouragement towards their spiritual growth is vital.'

Nearly all the responses could be slotted into three basic categories, suggesting that people saw their godparenting role in terms of their support of the parents, their relationship with the godchild and their particular responsibility to do with the spiritual side, with matters of faith. In *Children and Divorce*, Roger Smith and John Bradford summarise the duties of godparents as follows:

○ To represent the Church
  - through embodying the welcome of the Body of Christ;
  - through being a 'bridge of belonging' between Church and child;
  - through sincerity, thankfulness, thoughtfulness and fun.

○ To support the parents
  - through lasting friendship;
  - through affirming good patterns of parenting;
  - through endorsing their links with the household of God.

○ To encourage their godchild
  - through play, story-telling, games, activities and talk;
  - through private prayer (especially at baptismal anniversary);
  - through ongoing contact, dependability and availability.

Chapter 2 looked in much greater detail at the role of a godparent. To sum up, being a godparent means:

On the day, being part of the 'cast' at the godchild's baptism and making promises to support the parents in the Christian upbringing of their child.

Before, on and after the day, supporting the parents in other ways too.

Over the years, getting to know and relating to your godchild, helping him/her to feel 'special' as s/he grows up, and taking particular responsibility and concern for her/his development in faith – hopefully, developing an ongoing special friendship with him/her as an adult.

In the future, to 'be there' for the godchild if and when the parents are not or cannot be for any reason – to be another 'special' adult in his/her life. Having said this, it is important to repeat that becoming a godparent does not automatically mean that you commit yourself to being a child's guardian in the event of the death of the child's parents. If you are a very close and trusted friend or relative it may be that this is one of the reasons why you are invited to become a godparent. If so, it needs to be clearly stated and understood at the time and made abundantly clear, e.g. by inclusion in a parent's will.

Postscript

We set out to write this short book convinced of the importance of godparents in the lives of children. This conviction came from our own experiences both of being godparents and of being godparented. It was also influenced by our knowledge of children and families today and by our understandings of the churches to which we belong and their ministries with children. We felt that the subject did not have a high profile at present and that few people have written about it in recent years. Yet every week new godparents are making promises to encourage and support children in their nurture towards Christian maturity. They follow in a tradition that has proved helpful to both children and their families for almost two thousand years. In these days of small households, lack of community and religious plurality, it may be that responsible godparenting is about to become even more significant. Certainly godparents and issues related to them seem to pop up more frequently than perhaps they did and in some unusual places.

In the week of writing this postscript one of us has received an invitation to an infant baptism, had a long telephone call with an eighty-eight-year-old god-mum while arranging to spend Easter Day with her, and had a meal with some godchildren who are now young adults. Standing in the supermarket queue just yesterday a young mother, with two children in trolley seats and the rest full of foodstuffs, explained that her children were to be baptised on Easter Day 2000 and that family and friends would be travelling from 'all over the country' to join them. 'We've been going to church for some time now,' she said, 'but it seemed right to wait a little while and to have both children baptised together at a time when our families and friends could join us and the godparents.' She was thrilled that the church was organising an Easter egg hunt for the children. To her it was a sign that they were really being welcomed into their Christian community and to be welcomed and receive the sign of the cross on Easter Day is really special.

Hopefully this stranger's children will sense something of the joy and wonder of the Easter message and go on to develop relationships with their godparents that enable them to grow knowing that their godparents are alongside or there for them. Children need people in addition to their parents and close family who are significant role models, who make them feel special, who are bearers of the Good News as they love and care, and convey values and beliefs in line with the Christian faith. Through the rough and tumble of a loving relationship, godparents are in a good, perhaps godly, place to be disciple-makers. In so doing they are responding to two calls that Jesus made – one was to let the children come to him and the other was to make and baptise disciples.

Just by 'being there', sometimes across the miles by using the telephone or e-mail, godparents can be part of the child's community, providing models and experiences of the Christian faith in action. As the relationship develops and the child grows, it is to this anchor-person that the godchild may come with difficult questions or merely to talk about things that are difficult to chat to parents about. As one teenager put it: *'Do you mind if I talk to you? I have a question. Why is it that I find it more difficult to get on with my Dad now that I am a teenager?'* With a silent prayer for help, the godparent listened and enabled the godson to gain a glimpse into his father's situation. Being a parent, especially a parent of a teenager, can be tough and this teenager began to realise that while he faced the challenges of leaving home, his Dad faced the challenges of letting him go. Once through the teenage years the godson and his Dad got along well. Thanks to the godparent the godchild received support at just the right time from a person who had been there as long as he could remember – someone chosen by his parents to do just that. God had helped this godparent. No doubt, the godparents of the two children to be baptised on Easter Day will find that they are helped too.

It is with God's help that godparents fulfil their vital role in children's lives. May God bless them and encourage them through the support they receive from his Church.

A Prayer for Godparents ...

God and Father of us all, we pray for those who have under-taken the responsibility of serving as godparents.

Help them by your grace to fulfil their duties, and keep them faithful in prayer; that their godchildren may grow up in the knowledge of your love and in the faith of our Lord Jesus Christ, to serve and worship you all their days in the fellowship of the Church, to the glory of your name.

New Parish Prayers, edited by Frank Colquhoun,
Hodder and Stoughton, 1982.

... And a Godparent's Prayer

Father of all,
I pray for N..., my godchild,
and for his/her family.
Watch over him/her this day.
Grant N...
love and security in his/her growth,
a welcome in your Church,
joy and constructiveness in living,
the spirit of friendship, and the gift of health;
through Jesus Christ our Lord.
Amen

John Bradford

Resources

Albans, Helen: *Praying with Sticky Fingers* (Methodist Publishing House, 1992) – exploring prayer with very young children.

Bradford, John and Smith, Roger: *Children and Divorce* (National Society/Church House Publishing, 1997)

Hall, Christine Elliott, Jarvis, Judy and Jefferson, Mary: *It's a very Special Day* (National Christian Education Council, 1998) – creative ideas for celebrating the Christian year at home.

Hall, Christine Elliott, Jarvis, Judy and Jefferson, Mary: *Milestones* (Methodist Publishing House, 1993) – practical ways of marking important moments in family life.

Legood, Giles and Markham, Ian: *The Godparents' Handbook* (SPCK, 1997)

Whitehead, Hazel and Whitehead, Nick: *Baptism Matters* (National Society/Church House Publishing, 1998)

Becoming a Godparent: a guide for godparents and parents (National Society/Church House Publishing) – leaflet.

Common Worship Initiation Services (Central Finance Board of the Church of England, 1997, 1998) – provides a further account of the significance of baptism for the Church.

First Steps in the Church (Methodist Publishing House, 1992) – a booklet to help churches think through their approach to families with young children.

First Steps thank you card for godparents (Methodist Publishing House)

For a Godparent card (SPCK)

How Faith Grows (National Society/Church House Publishing, 1991) – a look at faith development and Christian education.

Something to Celebrate: Valuing Families in Church and Society (Church House Publishing, 1995)

Supporting Families (The Stationery Office, 1998)

Family Caring Trust, 8 Ashtree Enterprise Park, Newry, County Down BT34 1BY, 01693 64174 – publishes parenting courses for use by churches and other community groups.

FAITH in THE FUTURE

Other books in this series

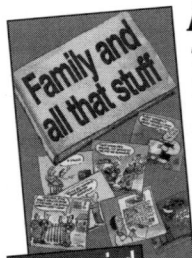

Family and all that stuff

TRUE stories by over 20 well-known Christians about their family lives, past and present. Fascinating human interest stories, illustrating some impressive mental and faith journeys – including some that involve considerable risk-taking.

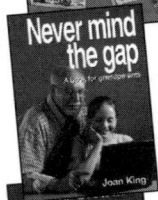

Never mind the gap

Explore the challenge and adventure of being a grandparent in today's society. This acclaimed title by Joan King includes activities, reflections and ideas to help you make the most of this significant relationship.

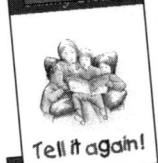

Tell it again!

Explore story-telling and creative games with young children. Michèle Taylor offers advice, background and a comprehensive set of resources including games, rhymes and stories.

Happy ever after

Explore the ways of nurturing and sustaining a marriage. Hugh Buckingham also considers the similarities and differences between formal marriages, recognized by Church and State, and informal marriages or committed cohabitation.

Breaking up is hard to do

Patrick Bond pays tribute to all marriages where people try hard and honestly to do the best they can. But primarily, he offers support and information for those who do come to the moment of breaking up. Discover the positive elements of the experience – beyond the collapse of ideal hopes, beyond mere survival and beyond bitterness and recrimination.

National Christian Education Council
1020 Bristol Road, Selly Oak, Birmingham B29 6LB.
Tel: 0121 472 4242   *Fax:* 0121 472 7575
E-mail: sales@ncec.org.uk   *Web site:* www.ncec.org.uk